The Best Wedding Shower Book

A Complete Guide for Party Planners

Courtney Cooke

Meadowbrook

Distributed by Simon & Schuster
New York

Library of Congress Cataloging-In-Publication Data

Cooke, Courtney
   The best wedding shower book.
   1. Showers (Parties) — planning. 2. Weddings —
I. Title

GV1472.7.S5C67   1987   793.2   87-5599

Published by Meadowbrook Press, 5451 Smetana Drive, Minnetonka, MN 55343

Page 44, "Mother Murphy II," Copyright © 1986 by Bruce Lansky. Reprinted from *Mother Murphy's 2nd Law* with permission of its publisher, Meadowbrook, Inc.

Page 51, "Magic Finger Jello," Copyright © 1974 by Vicki Lansky et al. Reprinted from *Feed Me! I'm Yours* with permission of its publisher, Meadowbrook, Inc. (Revised edition, May 1976).

The cartoons on pages 104 - 108 were excerpted from *Mother Murphy's Second Law* by Bruce Lansky © Copyright 1987, with permission of its publisher, Meadowbrook, Inc.

BOOK TRADE DISTRIBUTION by Simon and Schuster, a division of Simon & Schuster, Inc., 1230 Avenue of the Americas, New York, NY 10020.

S&S Ordering # 0-671-64171-9

Publishers ISBN # 0-88166-096-5 (priced)

99   98   97   14

Printed in the United States of America.

Editorial Director: Bruce Lansky
Editor: Sue Freese
Researcher: Lana Harris
Writer: Christine Larsen
Art Direction: Nancy MacLean
Text Design: Linda Lawson, Jill Rogers
Cover Design: Nancy MacLean, April Grande
Illustrator: April Grande, Bob Flaten
Keyline: Bob Flaten
Production: Nanci Jean Stoddard

Table of Contents

Introduction

Your closest friend calls with exciting news: She's getting married! There are many details to discuss, and in the heat of the moment, you say you'd *love* to give her a wedding shower. Then you hang up the phone, and panic sets in. You *hate* showers. Only your mother's friends really enjoy them. But you are the logical person to give the shower, and besides, you can't back out now. Is there a way to make this tired, old cliché interesting and fun? Absolutely!

Today's bride is dramatically different than her counterpart of even ten years ago. She's older and better educated, and she may have been supporting herself for some time. She may already have many household necessities—in fact, she may have been married before. The traditional "hen party" showers of yesteryear no longer seem appropriate.

But the reasons for giving a shower haven't changed at all. A shower is, above all, a celebration. It recognizes the beginning of a new household, a new partnership, and a new lifestyle for the bride and groom.

A shower is also an expression of support and encouragement—both material and emotional. As friends and family gather to offer household gifts, bits of wisdom and advice are also exchanged.

When you think about it, it's only the *trappings* of a traditional shower that you dislike: silly games, fussy decorations, fattening foods. *The Best Wedding Shower Book* will help you put aside the superficial paraphernalia and plan a meaningful celebration that's fun for you, your guests, the bride, and possibly the groom.

We've created a handbook of practical ideas for you. You'll find time- and money-saving ideas for decorating and food; innovative gifts; and entertaining alternatives to silly games. We've included men in our shower plans—they're part of all this, too. And we've also addressed such concerns as second and third marriages.

This book will show you how to plan a fun, memorable shower—without panic.

Why Give a Wedding Shower?

Chapter One

Although showers have been around for a long time, no one is sure when the custom originated. The idea of "showering" a bride-to-be with gifts seems to have its roots in Holland. One version of a Dutch folktale tells of a wealthy, young woman who fell in love with a poor miller. Her father forbade the marriage and denied the couple a dowry if they insisted on marrying. So the townspeople, sympathetic to this young couple, donated gifts to help them set up housekeeping.

There are countless variations of this story. And while the details may differ, the result is the same: The people of the town rallied to support the young couple. And showers remain an excellent way to help a new couple get off to a good start.

Bridal showers were popular with American "society women" by the turn of the century and were often given as surprise parties. Women's magazines of the day described elaborate menus and decorations. Activities probably included word games and puzzles, which were popular at that time.

The way we live and entertain is much more casual today than things were eighty years ago. For some reason, though, showers haven't changed much. Remember that a shower is a *party*, where you and your guests enjoy yourselves while offering gifts and encouragement to the bride. So plan foods you like and activities you enjoy (which may or may not be wedding related), and feel free to *i*nclude the groom and other male guests.

When Should a Shower be Given?

Showers once were women's affairs, given only for first-time brides. Today, the guest list often includes men; parties for couples are common, and men-only showers may even be given for grooms. What's more, showers are now often given for second- and even third-time brides. (Why not honor every new beginning in a positive way?)

An "unwedding" or divorce shower, tactfully presented, can give a terrific boost to a friend to help him or her recover from a divorce, both emotionally and materially. Celebrating the divorce may not be appropriate, but it is definitely appropriate to celebrate your friendship and show your support for your friend in a positive, fun way.

Many women today don't marry, either because of circumstances or by choice. If you and your friends are confirmed "bachelorettes," hold one or a series of parties for yourselves to celebrate (rather than bemoan) your singleness. You might even select a china pattern or start fresh with a matched set of bath linens or kitchen accessories. (Many stores are, in fact, encouraging singles to register for china and silver patterns.)

In a similar vein, women who have been married a long time can treat themselves to an "old wives' " shower. Friends exchange frivolous or humorous household gifts as they spend an evening or a lunch hour together.

Feel free to "shower" a friend or family member whenever an appropriate situation arises: going away to college, moving into a first apartment or first house, leaving on an extended trip abroad. Celebrating any new beginning can turn it into a cherished memory.

Who Should Host the Shower?

Generally, someone who feels close to the bride and groom, other than an immediate family member, gives the shower: an aunt, a cousin, a close friend, a close friend of the bride's or groom's mother. It is in poor taste for the bride's or groom's mother or sister to give such a party, because it seems too much like a plea for more gifts. If no one else offers to give a shower, a member of the wedding party should.

Chapter Two Planning Your Shower

Whether you plan to have a large, catered dinner for forty or an intimate gathering of six of your closest friends, the key to a successful, fun party is *careful planning*. After all, if everything else runs perfectly, but you forget to pick up the centerpiece, *that's* what you'll remember.

In addition, if you've planned well, you'll be more efficient and relaxed, the party will run more smoothly, and you will avoid last-minute headaches. So plan carefully, and as you think of details, write them down, so you won't forget them.

Setting the Date

Your first step is to set a date and a time for the party. Ask the bride (and the groom, if he's included) what date is most convenient for her. Her schedule will be hectic just prior to her wedding, and this should be your first consideration.

You can also anticipate scheduling problems for guests. Most wedding showers are held a month or so before the wedding; avoid scheduling your shower less than two weeks before the big event, or you're likely to have a very harried bride on your hands. It is also more difficult for the bride to get shower thank-yous out promptly when she's handling other last-minute details.

You may have other scheduling problems if your guest list includes people who plan to travel a considerable distance for the wedding. In that case, you will need to hold your party when they are in town, and may not be able to avoid eleventh-hour scheduling.

Don't forget to consult the calendar and note any major holidays or school vacations. Whether you schedule your party while school is in session depends on your guest list. Consider children you'd like to invite who couldn't come during school hours and mothers who may need to hire sitters during school vacations.

The Guest List

Begin organizing your guest list by consulting the bride and/or groom. Anyone who knows the bride or groom well and will be invited to the wedding is a potential shower guest. The bride or her mother are usually happy to furnish you with a list of names, addresses, and phone numbers. Ask for this information when you decide on the date and time.

You have a ready-made guest list for your shower if you know the bride through a club or an organization, if you work with her, or if you have a group of mutual friends. You're a fortunate hostess: All your guests know each other and presumably enjoy one another's company. But always consult the bride beforehand; she may know of someone else you need to invite or someone who may be feeling "tapped out" from attending several showers.

A note about surprises: They are *not* recommended. A bride-to-be has too many things to take care of just prior to her wedding to have unscheduled time, and you risk a potential disaster by planning a surprise shower. Save the surprise for another party.

The Invitations

Depending on the circumstances, you can mail written invitations, or you can phone. If the guest list includes just close friends or co-workers, word-of-mouth works just fine. If a group is giving the shower together, as in the case of a painting and decorating party, written invitations are silly; you simply need to coordinate the party by phone. If the party requires a detailed verbal explanation of the plans, such as a "roast," a phoned invitation is preferable.

However, a written invitation is in order if you do not know the other guests well. Likewise, if you need to include a map with directions to your house or circulate a detailed "wish list" of the bride's preferred gifts, send out written invitations.

Be sure to include the date and time of the party; the bride's (and/or groom's) name; preferred gift colors and sizes; your name, address (along with any necessary directions), and phone; and RSVP information. If you write "RSVP" at the bottom of your invitation, all invited guests are expected to notify you whether they can attend. If you write "Regrets only" at the bottom, it is understood they need notify you only if they cannot attend; assume anyone not heard from will be attending.

Write your invitation on personal stationery or on purchased, printed invitations. Or make your own invitations using the ideas in this book or your own ideas. Be sure to send the invitations early enough that your guests have at least two weeks to arrange their schedules and to shop for gifts.

Do's and Don't's

1. **Do** plan ahead; get your invitations out early.

2. **Do** take time before the party to get organized so the party will run smoothly. Then you'll have time to enjoy it, too.

3. **Do** consider including men.

4. **Don't** surprise the bride.

5. **Do** have fun with festive decorations. Consider useful decorations or centerpieces incorporating kitchen gadgets or fancy linens that can be presented to the bride at the end of the party.

6. **Do** include a bunch of bright balloons outside your door to greet guests as they arrive.

7. **Do** use your best table linens and silver if the party isn't too big. Save the matching paper plate ensembles for larger parties or for when you don't have time to wash linens and china.

8. **Do** present foods attractively; include garnishes.

9. **Do** know the diet restrictions of your group when planning your menu. If you plan to serve alcoholic beverages or calorie-laden sweets, provide alternatives for those who can't or don't choose to have them.

10. **Do** serve foods that are easy to eat.

11. **Don't** expect people to balance a sit-down meal on their laps.

12. **Do** have one or two detail-minded people sitting near the bride (or bride and groom) to handle wrappings and to record the gifts received.

13. **Don't** give only utilitarian gifts—consider something humorous or fun to help relieve prewedding tensions.

14. **Do** remember to invite the members of the wedding party and the mothers of the bride and groom as a courtesy.

15. **Do** keep the shower short and sweet.

16. **Do** use the bride's wedding colors in your decorating.

17. **Don't** play games that are embarrassing or awkward.

18. **Do** plan activities that guests will find truly enjoyable and that serve some useful purpose.

19. **Do** select useful prizes for guests.

20. Finally, **do** have a good time!

Checklist

Follow a checklist to help you plan; copy the list below. Checking off each task as you complete it leaves you free to concentrate on other details. If you plan to serve more than punch and a few munchies, write down your menu and post it in a handy spot in your kitchen. Such a reminder is helpful as you plan your shopping list and prepare the food. It will also keep you from forgetting that elegant molded salad waiting in your refrigerator!

Two months before the wedding
- ☐ Set time and date with bride and groom
- ☐ Prepare guest list

Three weeks before the party
- ☐ Decide on theme (optional)
- ☐ Make or purchase invitations

Two to three weeks before the party
- ☐ Send invitations
- ☐ Plan menu
- ☐ Plan activities and prizes
- ☐ Decide on your gift (Allow more time if you plan to make your gift)

One to two weeks before the party
- ☐ Make or purchase decorations
- ☐ Purchase your gift (Wrap it now, so you don't leave it until the last minute!)
- ☐ Prepare shopping list for all menu ingredients

One week before the party
- ☐ Check to see that all appropriate serving dishes and utensils are clean and on hand
- ☐ Check tables and folding chairs to be sure enough are on hand and in good repair
- ☐ Check table linens, wash and iron if necessary

Three days before the party
- ☐ Buy all groceries, except fresh bread and rolls
- ☐ Order centerpiece and other fresh flowers
- ☐ Clean house

The day before the party

- ☐ Prepare as much of your menu as possible
- ☐ Set table; decorate party room
- ☐ Bring chairs and tables out of storage; set up if possible
- ☐ Assemble paraphernalia for activities
- ☐ Wrap prizes
- ☐ Make sure your gift is wrapped

The day of the party

- ☐ Arrange your centerpiece or pick it up at the florist
- ☐ Purchase fresh bread and rolls
- ☐ Set out coasters and ashtrays
- ☐ Do last-minute dusting and vacuuming
- ☐ Prepare rest of the menu
- ☐ Set out a box and paper bag to handle gifts and wrappings

Last-minute details

- ☐ Get dressed at least thirty minutes to one hour before guests are expected (Don't be surprised by an early arrival!)
- ☐ Have coffee ready to brew; make sure other beverages are ready
- ☐ Greet your first guests and have a good time!

Chapter Three Choosing a Theme

Planning your shower around a theme is optional, but it does help provide a *focus* for the party's activities, menu, invitations, and decorations. A theme also aids the guests by narrowing their gift choices, making selection easier. A simple theme is the most workable and provides the most options for you and your guests.

Consider how all of the details of the shower can be tied to the theme:

Activities

Some themes suggest certain games or activities, lending purpose to the event. If your theme suggests no such activity, choose one from Chapter 4.

Invitations, Nametags, Placecards

Choose one of the invitation ideas described in the appendix, or create one of your own. Purchased, printed shower invitations are fine, too, as are simple notes written on personal stationery. The object of a written invitation is not only to clearly communicate the necessary information about the party but also to impart a festive mood.

If your guests don't know each other, adapt the invitation design to your nametags and placecards. Of course, guests who are already good friends do not require nametags, and placecards are just in the way at such a party.

Food

Your menu depends less on your theme than on the time of day your party is held and the number and type of guests you invite. But keep your theme in mind as you select serving pieces, linens, and other table decorations.

Decorations

Some themes suggest specific decorating ideas; others require simple decorations like colorful balloon bouquets, flowers, or crepe paper streamers. You may wish to attach a bouquet of balloons near your front door for a festive atmosphere as guests arrive.

Decorate as much or as little as you wish, depending on your available time and your budget. While festive decorations help create a festive atmosphere, they're not necessary for a successful party.

If you're trying to decide whether to spend your money and time on decorations or a more elaborate gift for the bride, do *both* by making a centerpiece from a pretty basket filled with useful wooden spoons, bowl scrapers, and artfully arranged colored dish towels. Or make a balloon bouquet at the chair you've set aside for the bride and attach a lacy blue garter to it. At the end of the party, present these decorative touches to the bride as part of her gift.

Provide a corsage for the bride to make her feel special. Make one from a lacy handkerchief and some silk flowers, tied with a pretty ribbon, or be whimsical and tie a small kitchen gadget to a pretty dishcloth.

Decorating tip: When choosing colors for balloons, paper napkins, or any other decorations, use the bride's colors.

The Party is the Gift

Some showers can be planned around a specific activity, such that the party itself provides a useful part or all of the gift. The warm memories of any shower are certainly a gift to the bride and/or groom. But you can take the idea a step further by planning activities that are not only fun but productive as well. Many of these ideas are particularly well suited to couples' parties.

Helping Shower

This party takes many forms but usually involves close friends of the bride gathering to help her prepare for the wedding. You may get together to address invitations or to decorate the bride's home or the reception hall.

Activity Be sure to choose an activity that can be accomplished by the number of guests invited in the time allotted.

Food Select food for its simplicity and portability. If you are addressing wedding invitations, serve the food after you finish and put away the invitations.

Decorations Since the purpose of this party is to accomplish a useful task, decorations other than a simple basket of flowers on the food table are unnecessary.

Quilting Bee

This is an old idea, but it's still fun if your guests are stitchers.

Activity A quilting bee can be organized in several ways. If you have plenty of time in advance, furnish guests with a square of fabric, chosen to complement the bride's decorating scheme, and complete instructions. Decide beforehand whether squares should be appliqued, embroidered, or stenciled, or whether each guest may choose which technique(s) to use. Specify the color scheme to be used, if you have one. Ask the guests to complete their squares and return them to you well in advance of the party.

Then, if you are ambitious, you can piece the squares and quilt them yourself. Or, if you have access to a quilt frame and a room large enough to accommodate it (and if your guests are equal to the task), you can hold an authentic quilting bee.

If there isn't time enough to assemble the quilt before the party, have each guest wrap her square, and present them to the bride at the party. Afterwards, you can finish the quilt yourself or have it done professionally. The disadvantage of this arrangement is that you might put it off or forget it, and the guests won't get a chance to see the completed quilt.

Invitations   Since you'll have to provide directions for preparing the quilt squares, written invitations are a good idea. Be sure to get the invitations out early, so your guests will have plenty of time to finish their squares. See the patchwork invitation in the appendix.

Food   Choose any menu suitable for the time of day. If you'll be sewing at the party, serve the food at the end of the party, after the sewing has been safely put away.

Decorations   Decorations will be in the way at this party, if you are sewing. Your sewing paraphernalia, neatly arranged around the room, is sufficient to create atmosphere. If you plan to present a completed gift, the same accessories, perhaps accented with a bow or some flowers (such as a wicker sewing basket, filled with dried or silk flowers), are appropriate.

Lingerie Party

Lingerie parties, usually attended by the bride's close friends, have become very popular. They are especially appropriate for a second wedding—and fun, too!

Activity   A home-party consultant comes to the hostess' home with samples of lingerie and other items. Sometimes, the guests model the lingerie. After the merchandise is shown, the bride leaves the room and the guests make their purchases. The lingerie is presented to the bride at the party, or the hostess delivers the gifts to her later.

Invitations   See the lacy invitation in the appendix.

Food

This party is usually held in the evening, so you can serve a dinner or after-dinner munchies or desserts. Or serve a selection of fancy after-dinner drinks and liqueurs or a variety of exotic coffees.

Decorations

Use satin ribbons and pretty scraps of lace in your decorating. Gather lace into a bunch shaped like a bouquet of flowers, and tie it with ribbon; tuck these bunches into plants, on tables, wherever there's an empty corner. Tie ribbon bows on the handle of a basket and fill it with puffs of lace for an easy, pretty centerpiece.

Painting/Decorating/Gardening/ Landscaping Party

This is a perfect opportunity to get the guys involved.

Activity

Everyone comes dressed to work and brings the appropriate tools: paint brushes, rollers, wallpapering tools, or gardening tools—whatever the situation requires. Expertise and elbow grease are the greatest gifts given at this shower, but guests may also purchase tools for the couple or pool resources to pay for materials. This fun party is an occasion you and your friends will thoroughly enjoy and remember for years.

Invitations

If you're giving guests instructions on what to bring, written invitations are in order. See the house invitation design in the appendix.

Food

Guests work hard at this party and should have a substantial meal when the work is done or during a break in the action. A potluck meal is best—each guest brings a salad, a casserole, a beverage, or a dessert. Coordinate the menu to ensure variety, and don't forget to supply disposable plates, cups, flatware, serving pieces, and trash bags for cleaning up.

Decorations

Because this is a working party, decorations other than a simple centerpiece are in the way.

Sewing Bee/Trousseau Party

This is another old idea; it requires guests who are experienced seamstresses.

Activity

You need a large room with several electrical outlets. Provide several sewing machines, an iron and ironing board, a full-length mirror, and other necessary sewing supplies. You and your friends then gather for an afternoon or evening of sewing—to help the bride make her wedding dress, an outfit for her trousseau, or something for her home.

In addition to expertise and effort, each guest may contribute fabric, a pretty piece of trim, or special buttons to the project. Or each guest can bring a few items to furnish the bride's sewing basket, which you provide. If you make the wedding dress, the bride should furnish the pattern and materials.

Invitations

Again, if you're giving directions, send out written invitations. See the lacy invitation in the appendix.

Food

Be sure to keep the food table well away from the sewing activity or put away the sewing before any food is served.

Decorations

You'll have plenty of sewing paraphernalia in your work room, so confine your decorations to pretty bits of ribbons, lace, and fabric or fresh flowers on the food table. See the section on lingerie parties for more decorating ideas.

Long-distance Shower

If the bride lives out of town, hold a long-distance shower for her.

Activity

Invite mutual friends and ask them to bring unwrapped gifts. After everyone has seen the gifts, wrap them and put them into a large box, which you ship to the bride. Take pictures of the guests at the shower, taking care not to photograph any unopened gifts, and send a set of the prints to the bride in her box of gifts. During the party, call the bride long-distance so all the guests can talk to her.

Any nice shower gifts are appropriate, but they should be light and compact for shipping. Very fragile items are not a good idea. You can specify a certain type of gift, such as kitchen items or linens, or gifts that remind the bride of the giver, such as a distinctive picture frame from a friend who is an avid photographer. Cash gifts mail well, too, and are always a good fit. (See the "money tree," page 30.)

Invitations	See the telephone invitation in the appendix.
Food	Choose foods that allow a "sampling" to be wrapped and sent to the bride, so she can taste the treats you had at the shower while she enjoys the photos and opens her gifts.
Decorations	Include photographs of the bride or bride and groom in your decorations. For fun, have a photo enlarged to poster size, then hang it on the wall or prop it on a chair and decorate it with flowers, netting, or ribbons. Use this poster to toast the bride at the party.

Traditional Showers

Many of the old standby showers make the most sense for the traditional women-only guest list.

Activities	Try to devise a game or contest based on your theme. Suggestions are given for some of the themes that follow. Also see Chapter 4 for more activity ideas.
Invitations	When you're asking each guest to bring a specific item, it's best to send written invitations. Likewise, send out invitations if your guest list includes more than just close friends. Also, be sure to mention if and where the bride has registered to help guests with gift ideas.
Food	Your menu will depend on what time of day you have the shower and who you invite. Some ideas are included with the following themes. Also see Chapter 5 for food ideas.

Decorations   Since these parties often don't lend themselves to specific types of decorating, the simpler the better. Be free with flowers, lace, and bows, especially if the gifts are less than glamorous. And try to tie in your theme; a few suggestions follow.

Kitchen Showers

Kitchen showers take many forms; be as general or as specific as you wish. Some kitchen shower themes are suggested below; others you might try include brushes, cutlery, soaps—anything you use in the kitchen. The more showers a bride is given, the more specific you can be with your theme.

Spice

Each guest brings a spice, along with her favorite recipe using that spice and a serving piece or utensil used in preparing the recipe. It's a good idea to preassign spices so you get a good variety. Otherwise, you may get a lot of cinnamon!

Activity   Have a contest in which guests identify a series of unlabeled spices by looking, smelling, and even tasting. Award the guest with the most correct answers.

Decorations   Fill a basket or bowl with spices and silk flowers for a pretty centerpiece.

Breakfast

Give gifts for making or eating breakfast—waffle irons, egg cups, coffee mugs, and toasters.

Activity   Have an impromptu recipe contest, in which each guest writes out a favorite or foolproof breakfast recipe. Don't advertise the contest—guests are to do this from memory.

Food   This type of shower is excellent when done as a potluck brunch. Ask each guest to bring a specific type of food—a main dish, beverage, bread, or pastry. You should provide dishes, silverware, napkins, and basic condiments.

Gadget

Each guest must include some kind of kitchen gadget as part or all of her gift. For example, a cheese grater can accompany a quiche pan; a coffee grinder fills the bill by itself.

Activity   Tuck small gadgets around the room to create atmosphere; ask guests to name as many as they can at the end of the party. Offer a prize to the guest who spots the most gadgets or who knows the function of the most. Present the gadgets to the bride as part of your gift.

Powder Room Shower

Provide the couple with all the things they'll need to properly furnish their bath—towels, soaps, bath oils, rugs, shower curtain, and bath accessories.

Invitations   Send out written invitations that give the bride's bath colors. Also mention where the couple has registered for gifts.

Emergency

This catch-all category covers all gifts that can be used in some kind of emergency. Possibilities include a selection of canned goods in case of blizzards or other weather emergencies, a first-aid kit, candles with matches or flashlights for lights-out situations, or a travel sewing kit. If this does not offer enough options, select a general kitchen theme with the emergency idea optional. However, you may be surprised at your guests' ingenuity—someone may show up with a bottle of wine and a canned fruitcake for drop-in company!

Activity   Have guests come up with an "emergency scenario" in which their gift will come in handy. Have guests vote on the most original idea.

Decorations   Create your own emergency basket filled with chocolate attack remedies; use it on your table as a centerpiece, and give it to the bride later.

Linen Shower

This is a popular theme because everyone needs linens. The category includes bath towels, kitchen towels, bed linens, and table linens. For this type of shower, be sure to include bed sizes and color schemes for kitchen, bedroom, bath, and dining room.

Invitations   Since it's important that you specify sizes and colors, send out written invitations. Also include the stores at which the bride is registered for linens.

Decorations   Use your prettiest table linens wherever possible.

China and Glassware Shower

Any bride who has registered china and crystal patterns will welcome this kind of shower. It assures the couple of receiving more than just a few select pieces of their chosen patterns. In addition to china and crystal, gifts can include kitchen glassware and dishes, vases, and candleholders.

Guests who do not know the bride and groom well will appreciate having a registered gift list from which to select a gift. This is a good shower theme if your guests are not just close family and friends.

If the pieces the bride has chosen are pricey, several guests can combine their resources for a group gift.

Invitations   Send out written invitations and list the stores at which the bride is registered.

Basket Shower

A basket shower provides useful gifts and gives your guests a chance to be creative in their gift selections. Inform them, on the invitations, that this shower requires that they bring a gift *in* a basket or a gift that *is* a basket.

Gifts might include a set of decorative nesting baskets, a casserole dish with a basket server, a wastebasket or painted basket filled with guest towels and decorative soaps. Give the bride a wicker laundry basket, a hamper, or any large, decorative basket in which to place gifts both during and after the party.

Activity   Advertise a prize for the most creative gift. Have guests vote for the winner.

Invitations   See the "basket of good wishes" invitation in the appendix.

Food   Serve as many of your menu items in baskets as you can: rolls in a bread basket, a casserole in a basket server, a dessert on a wicker tray. Consider serving a pie with a basketweave top crust for dessert.

Decorations   Use baskets in your decorating. In addition to your large basket for gift holding, put flowers in a basket on your table and nuts or candies in small baskets around the room for nibbling.

Box Showers

These showers supply gifts—anything that comes in a box, including such things as laundry soap or macaroni. Or the idea can be stretched to include small appliances or a box of handkerchiefs.

Activity   Offer a prize for the gift that is boxed in the cleverest way; have guests vote for the winner. Give the bride a decorative storage box to hold the gifts at the shower and store blankets or other items later on.

Invitations   See the "mystery box" invitation in the appendix. Also, it may help the guests think of gift ideas if you include a few examples in your invitations. In particular, show the wide range of gifts that are possible in all price ranges.

Food   Serve as many items as you can that either come in boxes or are made from ingredients that come in boxes, keeping track of those ingredients. After the food has been served, ask guests to name as many of these items as they can. Give boxed prizes.

Decorations   Let the wrapped gift boxes in the room carry out your theme in your decorating.

Pound Shower

This shower is similar to a box shower but provides gifts that are measured by the pound—soap, candy, flour, and other staples. Consider giving the bride a kitchen scale.

Closet/Storage Shower

This shower provides all kinds of organizational items—drawer and closet organizers, food storage containers, garment storage bags. Although these items lack glamour, the bride and groom will appreciate them. If several guests want to combine resources on a gift, matched sets of garment bags, shoe organizers, scented drawer liners, and inflatable hangers are good ideas.

Invitations   If the bride and groom have registered at any department stores, they may have included such items on their list. Include store names with the invitations.

Domestic Shower

A domestic shower is probably the least glamorous of all showers, but the bucket, brooms, mops, and other cleaning items the bride receives are no less needed. Receiving these items as gifts allows the bride to spend her money on other things. And with a little creativity these gifts can be fun to open.

Activity

Offer a prize to the guest who can add the most glamour to her homely gift and have guests choose the winner. Also, have each guest write down her best cleaning tip to give to the bride. Share the tips among the guests.

Invitations

See the "mop-and-pail" invitation in the appendix, or opt for the fanciest purchased invitations you can find.

Decorations

To counteract the utilitarian aspect of the gifts, go all out in your decorating, using lots of flowers, ribbons, and lace. Add a touch of humor wherever possible: Make a corsage for the bride from a pretty dish towel, a fancy ribbon, and a pair of pink rubber gloves.

Holiday or Seasonal Shower

Although this idea can be fun and provide some unique and interesting gifts, it can also be a shopping nightmare at the wrong time of the year. Guests choose or are assigned a holiday, a month, or a season. They then select a gift appropriate to that time: a serving piece, a decorative item, or a utensil used in making a seasonal dish (such as a spritz press for making Christmas cookies). If your friends are avid bargain hunters who often find out-of-season buys, they may enjoy the challenge of this shower. If guests have trouble finding suitable gifts, suggest a serving piece to complement the bride's china pattern, accompanied by a holiday recipe for a food that is served in that dish.

Invitations

See the "four seasons" invitation in the appendix. If your party is just before a major holiday, use purchased invitations with a holiday theme, but be clear on the invitation that this is a shower so guests know that a gift is in order.

Food

Include dishes in your menu from various holidays or seasons of the year, using holiday linens and serving pieces.

Decorations

Follow the seasonal or holiday spirit in choosing colors, flowers, and other decorations.

Book Shower

At this shower, each guest brings a book she thinks will be helpful in married life. The choice can be restricted to cookbooks or can include books on gardening, sex, household hints, humor, or remodeling. The books may be accompanied by a related gift—a cookbook with cookie cutters tied to the package bow or a pair of gardening gloves and a spade with a book on gardening.

Bag-lady Shower

This idea works if your friends love to shop garage sales and you can hold the shower on a Thursday or Saturday morning in good weather. Give each guest a shopping bag and a set spending limit—say, two or five dollars. Tell them to spend no more than the limit and to assemble back at your house in one hour. When guests return, have each unpack her booty. The merchandise goes to the bride, of course. If guests wish, they may also bring a wrapped gift with them.

Activity   Give a prize for the cleverest assortment, the most useful gift, and the best bargain.

Food   Prepare a brunch that will be ready after the shoppers return and share their gifts. Time everything very carefully.

Couples' Showers and Second Weddings

Couples' showers and showers for second weddings are discussed together because second-wedding showers are likely to include couples. Both types of showers should emphasize romance.

Honeymoon Shower

The character of this shower varies greatly, depending on the couple's honeymoon plans. Sexy nightwear and a bottle of champagne would be just the things for a couple spending two weeks in Bermuda. But camping gear would be in order for a couple going hiking in the mountains. A perfect group gift for any honeymoon shower is a camera with film, certificates for free film processing, and several blank photo albums.

Invitations

For invitations, try to get promotional picture postcards of the area the couple will be visiting from a travel agent. Write your invitation on the back and mail one to each guest.

Food

Serve foods suggested by the honeymoon destination. If the newlyweds are going to Hawaii, have a luau; if Texas, serve a barbecue.

Decorations

Decorate with travel posters and brochures about the couple's honeymoon destination.

Honeymoon-at-Home Shower

Provide a terrific two weeks at home for a couple who does not plan to go away for a honeymoon. Gifts may include maid service, free laundry service, and gift certificates for romantic meals out. Include free babysitting if the couple already has children. This shower is perfectly suited to a group effort.

A less expensive idea is to provide homemade dinners for the couple to eat later (such as frozen lasagne) and to offer your own services as babysitter, laundress, or cleaning person.

Bride and Groom Shower

At this couples' event, women bring gifts (such as tools) for the groom, and men bring gifts (such as housewares) for the bride. As each gift is opened by the bride or groom, the giver must explain how he or she thinks the gift will be used. Record these entertaining answers for later fun.

Activity

Play your own version of "The Newlywed Game" or another similar couples game in which partners predict each other's responses to game questions. Offer a prize to the winning couple.

Invitations

See the bride and groom invitation in the appendix.

Decorations

Cut out pictures of brides and grooms from magazines, mount them on colored paper, and post them in the room to add to the mood. Put tiny plastic bride and groom figurines on the dessert cake. Add a touch of humor by dressing Barbie and Ken dolls as a bride and groom. Put them in a toy car with a "Just Married" sign on the back, trailing tiny doll shoes.

Barbecue

If the wedding is in the summer or early fall, stage a barbecue. Friends can contribute to a potluck in your backyard or at a favorite picnic spot. Gifts should include items used at a picnic or barbecue: a picnic basket, a barbecue grill and/or accessories, picnic ware. Friends can go in together and buy a more expensive gift, if they want to.

Activity

If everyone's up to it, plan a quick game of volleyball or another sport that all of the guests can play.

Invitations

If you have the shower at a local park or picnic area, include a good map and directions with the invitations.

Food

If you decide on a potluck, coordinate what each guest is to bring to assure a good variety and quantity of food. You should provide paper plates, cups, napkins, and plastic utensils.

Romance Shower

This shower provides items guests feel are conducive to keeping romance in the marriage. Gifts may include fine wine, albums or tapes of romantic music, concert tickets, or even a weekend in a good hotel (especially if the couple has children).

Invitations

See the "hearts and flowers" invitation in the appendix, or use any flowery, romantic invitation. Valentine party invitations, if available, can be used if you clearly specify that this party is a shower.

Food

Plan a menu of romantic favorites. For instance, at an evening shower, serve a fancy dessert with a blended coffee or a variety of hors d'oeuvres and champagne.

Decorations

Put on soft, romantic music, and decorate with lots of lighted candles.

Gourmet Shower

A gourmet or tasting shower requires guests to bring a gourmet dish accompanied by the recipe and a serving dish or utensil used in preparing that dish. You provide the salad, wine, and other side dishes.

You can come up with many variations on this theme. For instance, have a pasta party in which gifts include a lasagne pan, a French bread basket, and a set of salad bowls. A beverage shower can include an espresso machine or wine glasses. A wine-tasting shower requires each couple to bring two identical bottles of wine—one for tasting and one for giving; you provide the cheese and other munchies.

Invitations

Where guests are asked to bring a food dish, it's a good idea to have them RSVP and tell you what they're planning to prepare. You may be able to avoid duplication or having ten desserts and no entrees.

Roast

This party is best when the bride, groom, and guests have all known one another for a long time—preferably since childhood.

Activity

Each guest stands and tells a humorous anecdote about the bride or groom and presents the couple with a related gift. For example, a guest begins, "My friend Bill, here, was always getting into trouble at school for playing hooky to go fishing. Well, I hope this keeps him from getting into trouble with Marcia" and hands the bride and groom his-and-hers fishing gear.

Invitations

Because of the complexity of this plan, invite your guests by phone so you can thoroughly explain the instructions. You may need to coordinate the gifts, in case everyone remembers old Bill fishing and Bill and Marcia receive more fishing tackle than they can use in three lifetimes. If such is the case, your friends can first select a gift and then concoct a fictitious story to go with it.

Decorations

Try to find some humorous memorabilia to use for decorations, like baby pictures of the bride and groom. Talk to the bride's and groom's parents about borrowing some such treasures.

Hobby or Sports Shower

If the bride or groom is a sports fanatic, you and your friends can help the new spouse learn to enjoy it, too, by providing him or her with skis, a bowling ball and shoes, or a book about the intricacies of sailing. If both the bride and groom enjoy a sport or hobby, supplement their equipment with a new tent, camera equipment, or whatever is appropriate.

Invitations

Folded notecards (such as those for thank-you notes) often come with sports-related designs on the front. Try to find some with an appropriate golf, sailing, or other sports theme, and write your invitation information on the inside.

Decorations

Use sports paraphernalia in your party room to help set the mood. Use your imagination: Set a bowling ball on the floor, and arrange silk or dried flowers in the holes, or prop a pair of canoe paddles in a corner and attach a bow and ribbon streamers. If your couple enjoys camping, replace the usual candles on your table with a camping lantern decorated with silk flowers. If you don't have access to the proper sporting equipment, arrange in advance with the other guests to use the party gifts as decorations.

Entertainment Shower

Provide the bride and groom with all manner of entertainment, such as their favorite records, movie or theater tickets, VCR tapes or membership in a VCR rental club, or the VCR machine itself as a group gift.

Activity

If you want to provide entertainment at this party, in addition to the gift opening and good conversation, consider renting and showing a favorite old movie classic. Or rent Miss Manners' wedding etiquette video.

Food

If you're showing a film, serve popcorn, soft drinks, and a variety of candies like those sold in theater concessions. If you plan a more substantial meal, serve your favorites, but write a fancy menu and post it on your buffet table. Give your menu items fun names, such as "Clark Gable Potatoes" or "Hollywood Ham Sandwiches."

Decorations

Hang posters or movie-magazine photos of various stars on your walls. Create a fanciful centerpiece using a green plant or floral arrangement. Cut photos of your favorite movie or music personalities from magazines; attach the photos to popsicle sticks and insert these "puppets" into the dirt or base of your arrangement. If photos of only the stars' heads are being used, tie little ribbon "bow ties" on the sticks for a more festive look.

Money Tree

This shower provides the gift that's always the right size and color. If the bride and groom are restoring an old house or building a new one, if they live out of town, or if they are hard to select gifts for, then a cash gift—tactfully offered—is probably the most useful.

Activity

Stand a tree branch in a large container filled with sand or gravel, or purchase a potted indoor tree. (Norfolk pine is a good choice, if gently handled.) As guests arrive, they each attach their gift anonymously to the branches of the tree with clothespins or paperclips.

If this is a long-distance shower and you will be mailing the money to the couple after the party, collect the money and convert it to a cashier's check later. Be sure to take a picture of the tree bedecked with money to send along with the gift to the bride and groom.

Groom's Showers

Who knows, this idea could catch on and replace the traditional stag party! A groom's shower might be given by the groom's male family members or by his friends to help him prepare for his new role as husband in a fun yet civilized way. The shower may be held concurrently with another party for his fiancee in a different part of the house.

Activity

Plan any activity you and your friends usually enjoy—play cards, go bowling, or sit back and watch your favorite sport on TV. If you wish, each guest can give a humorous or helpful description of his gift and how to use it.

Invitations

Because most men are unfamiliar with the concept of a shower, phone invitations are probably best. Be sure to explain that a gift is in order; specify the type of gift if it's part of the shower theme.

Food

Serve the foods you enjoy at any get-together: popcorn, beer, pizza, or any other snack foods. Make clean-up easy by using paper plates and plastic cups and silverware.

Decorations

Because these men's parties are likely to be very informal, special party decorations are not required.

Workshop Shower

Provide the groom with the basic tools he'll need to make everyday repairs and keep his home running smoothly, or give him power tools, if he's likely to use them. Organizers filled with a selection of nuts, bolts, and washers and how-to-do-it books are great, too.

Lawn and Garden Shower

This is a good shower idea if the couple has a new house with a yard to care for, since it's likely the groom doesn't have lawn care tools. Possible gifts include rakes, shovels, or even a lawnmower or snowblower.

Activity

Guests can supply the groom with their favorite lawn care tips—humorous or otherwise.

Personal Shower

This idea is mostly just for fun—to provide the groom with new socks, pajamas, and underwear to help him "clean up his act" before the bride gets him.

Cooking or Gadget Shower

Every man, whether married or single, needs to know at least the basics of cooking. It might be fun for the groom's mother and her friends (depending on their relationship with the groom) to give this shower to help the groom polish his culinary skills. If he's an inexperienced cook, cookbooks that explain techniques in detail are in order. Masculine aprons and the recipe for his favorite dish (from his mother), accompanied by the proper pan for cooking it, are also good ideas.

Family Showers

In addition to the more general women's and couples' themes, the following showers are particularly well suited to parties that include the bride's and groom's entire families.

Family Wisdom Shower

Building around the advice activities in the following chapter, have each guest bring a gift coordinated with his or her favorite hints. For example, someone with a clever hint for easy bedmaking might bring sheets; another guest who has a great trick for cleaning silver might bring a silver chest or polishing cloths.

Activity

As gifts are opened, ask each guest to relate his or her advice or hint. Have someone record these words of wisdom on the "keepsake scrapbook" (see appendix p. 109).

Invitations

Because you'll need to explain the nature of the gifts, you may want to telephone your invitations. Or provide your guests with written instructions and standardized forms on which to write their hints, enclosing them with written invitations.

Food

Serve the favorites your family traditionally serves on holidays and other special occasions. If you enjoy any ethnic specialties, this is a good time to serve them.

Decorations

Decorate with old and new family photographs, especially wedding pictures and albums.

Heirloom Shower

Each guest can bring the couple a family heirloom or a gift that is destined to become a treasured heirloom, such as a hand-stitched sampler or a hand-crocheted lace bedspread. Check with other family members first to be sure this won't be a hardship for them; if so, make the heirloom idea optional.

Activity
Encourage guests to relate stories concerning various family mementoes—where they came from, how they were used, or any other interesting family lore.

Food
Again, plan a menu of family favorites. Serve your food using as many family heirlooms as you can, including treasured table linens, china, and serving pieces.

Decorations
Ask guests to help you decorate with family mementoes and old photos in frames and albums.

Anniversary Shower

This shower is based on the old rule of anniversary gift giving: first year, paper; second year, tin; and so on. Each guest chooses a particular number and selects a gift appropriate for that many years' anniversary. For example, the guest who selects twenty-five brings an item made of silver; the one who chooses the number one brings an assortment of paper party goods. See the appendix for the complete listing of corresponding anniversaries and gifts.

Activity
When it's time for gifts to be opened, have each guest give his or her gift in numerical order, starting with the first anniversary. Tell the bride what gift category is represented by each particular anniversary (wood, glass, etc.) and encourage her to guess what's inside each package as she opens it.

Decorations
Decorate with old and new family photographs, especially those taken at weddings and anniversaries. Use anniversary decorations and banners available at stationery stores.

Showers with Co-workers or Close Friends

Showers given by a bride's co-workers or close friends can be lively, since the guests know each other well.

Personal Shower

Gift choices for a personal shower include lacy underthings, scented soaps, and perfume.

Invitations   See the lacy invitation or the lingerie invitation described in the appendix.

Decorations   Decorate with netting, pretty lace, and ribbons. (See the section on lingerie parties for more decorating ideas.)

Japanese Tea Party

Food   Provide a selection of exotic teas for tasting, along with an assortment of munchies. Guests may bring gifts of favorite teas, a china tea service, or a luncheon cloth with napkins.

Decorations   Decorate with Japanese lanterns, sit on the floor, and listen to Japanese music to set the mood. (Look for the music in your public library.)

Home Office Party

Help the bride set up an efficient home office with coordinated desk accessories, a file cabinet, desk lamp, or an assortment of paper supplies.

Invitations   Use the office memo invitation in the appendix.

"Stagette" or "Doe" Party

You guessed it! This is the female counterpart to the infamous stag party.

Activity

Some women think it's fun to hire a stripper or to go en masse to a male strip show. You can tame this idea down a bit by hiring some muscular, good-natured male friends to be topless waiters for the evening. Gifts may range from sexy lingerie and sex manuals to—well, use your imagination.

Paper Shower

If you work in an office, "pushing paper" all day, then try this idea for your shower. Guests bring gifts made only of paper: plates, cups, napkins, funny toilet paper—you may be surprised at the variety.

Decorations

This is one instance where you *should* make use of the coordinated paper party goods (tablecloths, napkins, plates, cups, and centerpieces) available in stationery stores. Hang pleated paper "wedding bells" and crepe paper streamers from chandeliers, curtain rods, or the ceiling to provide a festive atmosphere.

Other Showers

Divorce Shower

This is one case where a surprise can be fun. If your friend has come out badly in a divorce—emotionally, financially, or both—he or she may not feel much like shopping to replenish needed household goods. Arrange ahead of time with your friends to shop together or independently for the items your friend needs most. Arrange to meet at your divorced friend's home or have him/her come to your house. Inject humor into the situation wherever possible. (See "Roast," page 28.)

Invitations   It will be easier to coordinate this party over the phone. Be sure everyone knows it's a surprise!

Food   Serve your friend's favorites. You and your friends should supply all the food, beverages, paper plates, cups, and flatware.

Singles Shower

You don't have to be engaged to start acquiring pretty things for yourself. Schedule a party with your friends to exchange names and treat each other to something nice for your homes. Or plan a series of parties, each of you hosting a party for another in your circle of friends.

Food   Serve wedding reception foods: mints, nuts, finger sandwiches, and a tiered cake with a bunch of flowers or a figure of a woman dressed for success on the top.

"Old Wives' " Shower

After many years of marriage, every woman needs a lift. Give yourselves an "Old Wives' " shower to provide that boost. Exchange names among friends in advance or bring a wrapped gift to the party and take your chances. Gather at a friend's home or a nice restaurant to open gifts and enjoy each other's company.

Activity   See who can remember the most outrageous old wives' tale.

Invitations   Buy the prettiest shower invitations you can, or see the hearts and flowers or lacy invitations in the appendix.

Decorations   Treat yourselves to fancy and festive decorations. Feel free to use as many flowers, lace, netting, and pretty ribbons as your time and budget allow.

Chapter
Four
Keeping the Party Rolling

The activities you plan for your shower determine, in large part, how much fun the party is, so thoughtfully match activities to guests. Is a game even necessary? Good friends welcome the chance to catch up on conversation; planned activities may be in the way. On the other hand, if some or all of your guests are not already well acquainted, you'll need an icebreaker to get everyone talking. In this situation, a planned activity is essential to the success of your party.

The best party activity is one with a purpose—providing both fun and a useful gift at the same time. Choose activities that:

- encourage conversation and interaction among guests. Avoid written tests. Calling out verbal answers to guessing games is more fun; besides, trying to write on your lap while holding a glass of punch requires enormous balancing skill.

- are tasteful and do not make any of the attendees feel foolish or embarrassed. Games that get too personal or put people on the spot make many guests uncomfortable.

- are really fun. A good guideline: Would you consider playing this game at any other time?

The entertaining ideas presented in this chapter satisfy these requirements. They are organized to provide fun alternatives for any guest list. But, as with the themes shared in Chapter 3, most are also fun and workable for more than one category. So read them all before you decide.

Women-only Showers

Nametags

One popular icebreaker that gets people talking is based on nametags. Write the name of a fictitious character (one of a famous couple, perhaps, such as Romeo) or draw a wedding-related object (such as a bouquet or a garter) on each tag. As each guest arrives, attach the tag to her *back*, not allowing her to read what is written on the tag. (Be sure to remove mirrors from the room.) Guests ask each other "yes" or "no" questions to discover the identity of the "alter egos" on their nametags. Offer a prize to the first and last persons to guess correctly.

This game works well because it's fun and it gets the guests out of their chairs and talking to each other. It also helps guests learn each other's real names, enlivening later conversation.

General Advice

This game makes a terrific icebreaker. After all the guests have arrived, ask each to introduce herself and relate her best advice for a happy marriage. (Or you may ask for cooking or cleaning tips.) Ask one guest to record this wisdom for the bride to take home. A page is provided in the appendix for you to copy and use for this purpose. (See the "keepsake scrapbook" idea on page 109.)

What's the Bride Wearing?

Explain this activity to the bride in advance, so she knows what to expect. Allow your guests to visit awhile, then signal the bride to leave the room, so she's out of sight of guests, or cover her with a sheet (so she can hear what's said). Then ask questions of the guests: What color are the bride's shoes? Is she wearing a skirt or slacks—anything to test the guests' observation. Include as many questions as you can, adding more at the end about the bride's favorite color, movie star, or food. (Get the correct answers to these questions in advance.)

Avoid the pencil-and-paper pitfall by going around the room as in the previous game; everyone left "in" after you've asked all your questions wins a prize.

Singing Telegram

As a group activity, guests set their own words to the tune of "Here Comes the Bride" or some other appropriate tune; when the song is finished, serenade the bride together. Or write your own song ahead of time and arrange for a professional to sing your "telegram" at the party. Write down the bride's special song so she can keep it.

Couples' Showers and Second Weddings

Lovegram

Make a copy of the lovegram form in the appendix, mount it on cardboard, and decorate it with colored pencils or markers (if you wish). Hang it in a prominent spot. At the party, compose an anagram using the couple's names, preferably with a romantic theme. Give this poster to the bride and groom to take home.

Keeping Romance in the Marriage

Guests take turns telling the bride and groom their favorite hints for keeping a marriage exciting. Record this advice on a cassette tape or on the form provided in the appendix, and send it home with the bride and groom. (See the "keepsake scrapbook" on page 109.)

Couples Trivia

See the appendix for suitable "trivial" questions; add your own if you can. Divide your guests into two teams and take turns asking questions, or ask questions of the group at large. The first person to answer a question correctly gets a point. Give a prize to the individual or to each member of the team with the most points after all the questions have been asked.

Complete the Proverb

Read the first half of the proverbs in the appendix and ask guests to complete them—either with the real endings or humorous ones. Record the proverbs on cassette or use the form in the appendix for the bride and groom to keep.

Guess the Pasta

This is the perfect activity for a tasting/gourmet party. If a variety of pasta or wines (or other dishes) is served, number each and ask guests to identify them. Ask each guest to write his or her guess on paper and offer a prize to the person with the most correct (or the most creative) answers.

Best Wishes

Provide notecards and envelopes for guests to write happy thoughts for specific occasions. The suggested moment for opening the note should be written on the envelope: for example, first anniversary, wedding night, or after the couple's first fight.

Lover's Lane

Guests take turns relating their best tales (humorous ones) about lover's lanes or reminisce about their favorite romantic spots.

Famous Pairs	Put together a list of famous romantic pairs; get ideas from the trivia game questions in the appendix. Divide guests into two teams. A member of Team 1 names one of a famous pair of lovers; the first member of Team 2 two must then name the corresponding partner. If he or she cannot, the next member of Team 1 gets a chance. Teams get one point for each correct answer. Set a timer; at the end of a specified period, the team with the most points wins.
Love Dictionary I	Have a tape recorder handy for this one, if you can, or ask a guest to record the definitions on the form in the appendix. Ask guests to name typical endearments, like "honey," "dear," or "sweetie." Discuss possible definitions for what those words *really* mean. For example, "honey" may mean "I love you—I need help with the laundry" or "Guess what I bought today?" Send the cassette or written record of these definitions home with the bride and groom to refer to later. (See the "keepsake scrapbook" on page 109.)
Love Dictionary II	This activity involves making up a list of endearments for the couple to use in their marriage. The more creative or ridiculous the names ("passionflower," "snugglebunny," "lily-lips"), the funnier. Write them down on the pages furnished in the appendix or record them on tape for the couple to take home. (See the "keepsake scrapbook" on page 109.)
Roast	Ask guests to take turns telling their own stories about the couple. Encourage humorous, outrageous—but friendly—recollections. The longer guests have known the couple, the funnier the stories are likely to be. (See the "Roast" theme, page 28.)
Toast the Bride	Guests take turns toasting the bride and groom, offering their own best wishes. These wishes may be general or specific, serious or humorous, but all should be recorded for the bride and groom to take home.
Fun Ceremony	Write your own wedding ceremony just for fun, recording it on paper (see the appendix) or tape for the bride and groom to keep. Encourage the bride and groom to "practice" this ceremony at the party.

Dollar Dance	Hire musicians or borrow a good sound system and hold a dance. Include a "dollar dance": each woman dances for a minute or so with the groom and pays him a dollar for the privilege; male guests pay the bride for a dance. Collect the money and give it to the couple as a group gift.
Hot Tub	Rent a hot tub and have a backyard pool party. If this idea really appeals to you but your party is large, rent two or more tubs.
Boat Party	If you live near water, take advantage of it and hire a boat for an afternoon or evening. Bring along a picnic-style meal and plenty of snacks. If you serve alcoholic beverages, invite a nondrinking friend or hire someone to be the "designated driver." It's just as dangerous to drink and drive in a boat as it is in a car!

Groom's Showers

Advice on How to Keep Her Happy	Married guests may solicit this advice from their wives before the party. Ask each guest, in turn, to give his best advice to the groom. Advice can include ways to keep a woman happy, lawn and garden tips—even cooking tips. Record this wisdom on tape or on paper for the groom to keep and refer to as needed.
"How My Wedding Drove Me Crazy"	Ask guests to take turns relating anecdotes about humorous or frustrating events at their own weddings or those they've attended. To make these accounts more useful, encourage guests to offer their advice about how to cope (or how they managed) in a similar situation.

Family Showers

Marital Stability	Ask guests to take turns giving their best advice to the bride (and groom, if he's there) about how to keep life in the marriage: tips for cooking, cleaning, and anything else that helps keep a marriage or home running smoothly. Most interesting will be the tales the older generation can tell about how it was done in *their* day. Record the advice on tape or on the pages furnished in the appendix for the new couple to put to later use. (See the "keepsake scrapbook," page 109.)

Write Your Own Captions

Make copies of the cartoons in the appendix; post them on the walls of the party room or on the food table. As guests visit, have them write their own captions for each cartoon. Give the cartoons to the bride and/or groom at the end of the party.

Scrapbook

Purchase a scrapbook for the bride and groom. Plan several of the written activities in this book. Ask a guest to take lots of instant photos at the party. As activities are completed and photos are taken, mount the papers and photos in the scrapbook. As gifts are opened, put the cards in the book, too, next to a picture of that gift being opened. Present the scrapbook to the couple at the end of the party, as a starter book to fill and supplement with early marriage mementoes.

Traditions

Read selections from bridal traditions around the world in Chapter 7. Have guests discuss these traditions, as well as any that their family or friends may follow.

This Is Your Life

Pattern your shower after this old TV show. First, prepare a short slide show of the bride and groom when they were young. Or show family movies, if they're available. Next, include a "mystery guest." Choose someone who knew one or both of the couple in the past, preferably a long time ago. Have the mystery guest (or guests) hide while sharing some stories about the couple. Ask the bride or groom to identify the person who is talking about them—if they can. This is especially fun if you can include an unexpected—and *welcome*—acquaintance as your mystery guest. Record the event on video tape for a lasting souvenir.

The Firstborn Profile

Have your guests help you predict the attributes of the couple's first child, without knowing they're doing it.

As each guest arrives, ask him or her to name an item in a category so that you can fill out the baby profile form (see the appendix). The first guest should choose a sex, the second, a first name, the third, a middle name, and so on. To fill in hair- and eye-color blanks, ask someone to name any color. For the height blank, limit the possibilities to numbers between 54 and 84. Limit the weight answers to numbers between 95 and 300. Add more categories, if necessary, so that each guest can answer a question.

When the future baby's profile is complete, your guests will enjoy hearing that the couple's first child will be a female sumo wrestler who will have lavender eyes and cinnamon-colored hair, will be over six feet tall, but weigh only 103 pounds. Give a copy of the profile to the bride and/or groom to keep and contrast with the real baby later.

Showers with Co-workers and Close Friends

What the Bride Will Say

Because of the potential embarrassment to the bride, reserve this game for a group of the bride's closest friends. Ask one guest to unobtrusively write down everything the bride says as she opens her gifts. After all the gifts are opened, read her comments back to the group, explaining that these words describe the bride's reaction to her wedding night. In the right company, the resulting double entendres can be very funny. Give the bride the list to keep.

Lingerie Demo

If you're having a lingerie party, take turns modeling the lingerie and treat each other to a just-for-fun fashion show. Let yourselves get carried away, being as slinky and sexy as you can; try to include some fun patter: "Here's Denise in a scarlet, strapless silk peignoir. Notice how the fluid lines drape, accentuating every curve." If you have access to a movie or VCR camera and your guests don't mind, record this happening for posterity.

At the Movies

Take a page from the men's book and show racy movies. Or, on a more tame note, try a Tom Selleck or Richard Gere film festival.

Scavenger Hunt

Several hours before the party, stash several small gifts in bars or other night spots you and your friends frequent—get permission from the proprietors first. (If you want to be *really* mean, hide something in the men's room of a busy bar.) When you and your friends get together for your "night on the town," give the bride the list of places she must look for her booty.

"Last Chance"

Give the bride one last chance at her favorite movie star. Write a letter to him, several weeks before the party, requesting a signed photograph or letter on her behalf. (Keep a copy of your letter to the star to read at the party.) If her "heartthrob" answers your letter, read the response at the party, and, of course, give the letter to the bride. If there is no response, make one up yourself.

Male Stripper

For the ultimate in prewedding thrills, hire a male stripper to attend your function. Or attend a male strip show together. Carefully consider the sensitivities of all your guests—especially the bride—before planning this activity.

Divorce Shower

Belly Dancer

If your divorced friend is a man, consider hiring a belly dancer to entertain him and lift his spirits.

"Here's to You"

Make or purchase a guest book or poster and ask guests to write a wish for your friend in his or her new life. Present the book or poster to your friend as a group gift.

Mother Murphy II

Read a few bits of wisdom excerpted from *Mother Murphy's 2nd Law* by Bruce Lansky. Encourage guests to make up their own laws and record them in a notebook for the guest of honor. Here are some examples to get things rolling:

The Divorce Cause
To the best of anyone's knowledge, the leading cause of divorce is marriage.

The 50/50 Split
Fifty percent of all married couples get divorced. The other 50 percent are still fighting.

The Youth Factor
The younger you were when you got married, the younger you'll be when you get divorced.

The Divorce Doctrine
Divorce is a legal method for continuing a relationship you couldn't stand.

Singles' Showers

What's My Fortune?

In addition to most of the activity selections for close friends of the bride, a "mystery future" shower is lots of fun for a group of single women. Hire a gypsy fortune teller or tarot card reader or a ouija board. Guests can take turns asking questions about their own futures or that of the guest of honor.

Old Wives' Showers

Old Wives' Tales

Take turns remembering and relating the most ridiculous old wives' tales you and your friends ever heard. If your friends are stumped, ask, "What's the worst advice your mother or father ever gave you?"

Unstructured Activities

Who says you need any structured activity? Good friends need only good food, cheery, comfortable surroundings, and stimulating conversation, to have a good time.

If the conversation lags, throw in one of the following conversation starters informally, or ask each person in turn:

- How have weddings and marriage roles changed over the years?
- What's the funniest thing that ever happened at a wedding?
- What's the most frustrating part of being married?
- What's the best or worst advice for a new bride or groom?
- What went wrong on your honeymoon?
- What went wrong on your wedding night?

Prizes

Choose prizes that are both useful and a bit special. Spend a little more on a few nice prizes, rather than lots of cheap, useless ones, and keep your guest list in mind when selecting. Remember that, even within a group of close friends, tastes can vary dramatically, and since you have no idea who will win a particular prize, stick with universally well-received items. Some suggestions follow.

It doesn't hurt to have a few extra prizes on hand in case of ties. If you keep your receipts, you can return any extras after the shower.

Here are some good, basic shower prizes:

fun note/message pads or Post-it notes
shopping list pads
note cards or stationery
mugs (especially those with fun designs, like hearts or rainbows)
candy
small green plants in pots
bubblebath
refrigerator magnets
inexpensive napkin rings
heart-shaped ice cube trays (or other fun shapes)
magnetic picture frames
other plastic picture frames
coasters
padded hangers
fancy recipe cards
useful kitchen gadgets
fancy soaps

hand lotion
guest towels
pretty paper napkins and plates
cocktail napkins
a six-pack of beer or a bottle of wine
unusual pens
pocket organizers
mixed nuts
fancy office supplies, such as gold or multicolored paper clips
golf tees
fishing lures
tennis balls
plastic organizers (available in hardware stores, they come in various sizes to hold hardware, office supplies, sewing supplies and fishing tackle)
selected tidbits of imported foods from the supermarket

For more ideas, browse in a dime store, gift shop or the notions or stationery section of a department store.

Chapter Five **Serving the Food**

Good food is the common denominator of most successful parties; bridal showers are no exception. Don't limit yourself to those old standbys, sweet desserts and coffee, or the typical casserole/sweet roll/jello medley. Instead, serve the kinds of food you enjoy at any party.

Your major consideration when planning the menu is the time of day at which you'll have the party. The most popular times for showers are weekend noons, afternoons, and weekday evenings. Of these, only the weekend noon requires a full meal; at other times, serve a variety of snacks and/or desserts.

Your next consideration when planning the menu is your guest list. If you're serving thirty or forty guests, choose foods that require less individual attention than those you can handle when serving an intimate group of six. But whether you're serving six or thirty, choose recipes that can be prepared ahead of time, so you can get out of the kitchen and in on the fun when the party starts. Serve beverages that are prepared in quantity and served from a punchbowl or pitcher, rather than mixing individual glasses after the guests arrive.

If your group is too large to be accommodated comfortably at your table, don't serve a sit-down meal (that is, one that requires a knife). Don't expect guests to balance a tray (especially if it includes a cup of steaming coffee!) on their laps and cut meat or butter a roll—it's difficult to manage gracefully and invites disaster.

Instead, set out platters of finger foods—snack-size versions of your favorite dishes that can be eaten easily with your fingers, toothpicks, or a fork. These foods can be just as nutritious as any casserole—you can provide a fully balanced meal of these bite-size portions. And serving them has additional advantages:

- Conversation flows when guests gather around the table for snacking, providing an automatic icebreaker.

- You don't need to interrupt involved conversations to serve a meal.

- Guests don't feel obligated to eat a full meal.

- Serving your food in the individual disposable or edible containers recommended below means less dishwashing for you.

Be sure to consider any special dietary concerns your guests may have. And since almost any party is likely to have at least one dieting guest (possibly the bride!), be a sport and provide some low-calorie options.

Hors d'oeuvres and Snacks

Appetizers and snacks are probably the all-time favorite party foods, and they're welcome at showers, as well. Serve a selection of these tasty morsels at an afternoon or evening shower.

It's not hard to serve snack-size tidbits that are tastier and more nutritious than grocery store chips and dips. Experiment with your favorite recipes for sandwiches, salads, and other favorites to adapt them for snacking. You'll need to decrease baking times for the smaller sizes.

Caution: Don't plan to serve your experiments at the party, unless you can prepare the food far enough in advance to allow for disasters. Otherwise, you may need to make a fast trip to the deli!

In addition to the recipes that follow, consider trying these menu ideas:

- Bake your favorite casserole and present it in a single-serving "nest" made of:

A patty shell: You can buy these preformed pastry cups at a bakery or buy frozen ones and bake them.

A toast cup: Press square slices of bread into a muffin tin; toast in the oven until firm and golden.

A potato bird's nest: Purchase these ready-made or make them yourself. You'll need a special tool to hold the shredded potatos in form while you fry the nests.

- Serve your favorite salads in single-serving patty shells, toast cups, or bird's nests, too.

- Allow gelatin salads to set up a bit in your refrigerator; then spoon the gelatin into foil cupcake cups; garnish each. Guests can eat the jello directly from the cups.

- Make finger jello (usually recommended for toddlers) in a variety of shapes and colors—it's attractive, tasty, and easy for adults to eat, too. Make it more decorative and easier to handle by setting each piece on a small paper candy cup. Garnish with a squirt of mayonnaise or whipped cream. (See p. 51).

- Cut desserts and cakes in advance and set them into cupcake cups, or bake single servings in the cups to begin with. If you have access to plastic wedding cake tiers, arrange cupcakes, petit fours, or other individual desserts on the tiers to resemble a wedding cake.

Snack Bites

Make your favorite sandwich on slices of small cocktail rye or on quarter slices of bread. Or ask your bakery to slice a loaf the *long* way. Cut shapes into these large slices with cookie cutters; before removing the excess bread, spread filling on top. Remove the excess bread and filling from around the sandwich shapes, garnish, and arrange on a platter. Add to the platter folded, thinly sliced cheese and cold meats. Add another platter of vegetable sticks (carrots, celery, green pepper, and zucchini), deviled eggs, olives, and pickles for a complete "mini-meal."

Baby Burritos

Grated cheese
Grated onion
Chopped tomato
Shredded lettuce
Sliced black olives

Shredded or diced beef or chicken
(cooked)
Tortillas
Sauces for dipping

Use a combination of the above or your own favorite fillings. Cut tortillas into quarters and roll into tiny burritos. Top with sliced olives for garnish; serve with a variety of sauces for dipping: guacamole, sour cream, picante sauce.

Taco Dip

1 can (7 3/4 ounce) frozen avocado or
    guacamole dip, thawed, or
    refrigerated guacamole dip
1 1/2 cups chopped tomatoes

1 1/2 cups chopped lettuce
2 tablespoons chopped onion
1 1/2 cups shredded cheddar cheese (6
    ounces)

Spread dip on a tray or platter with sides. Sprinkle on the tray, in order: tomatoes, lettuce, onions, cheese. Serve with taco chips. Serves 6-8.

Enchiladas

10-12 flour tortillas
2 cans cream of chicken soup
1 pint sour cream
1 small can chopped mild green chilies
2 cups grated cheddar cheese

1 1/2 pounds ground beef, browned and
    drained
1 pouch taco seasoning
sliced ripe olives

Mix taco seasoning with ground beef, adding water according to the package directions. In a separate bowl, mix soup, sour cream, and chilies. Add half this mixture to beef mixture. Dip each tortilla in small amount of vegetable oil in a pie plate for a few seconds on both sides. Place beef and cheese on tortillas, reserving half the cheese; roll up. Place seam side down in ungreased 9″ × 13″ pan. Pour remaining sauce over top; cover with remaining cheese and sliced olives. Bake at 400° for 30 minutes. Serves 10-12.

Cucumber Sandwiches

2-3 cucumbers
8 ounces cream cheese, softened

1 loaf thin-sliced sandwich bread (white
    or rye)

Cut bread into circles using a cookie cutter or a tin can that's been opened on both ends. Spread bread with cream cheese. Top with a thin slice of cucumber. Serve chilled.

Water Chestnut Wraparounds

2 cans (8-ounce) whole water chestnuts, drained
1/4 cup soy sauce

2 tablespoons sugar
10 slices bacon
toothpicks

Cut water chestnuts in half; marinate in mixture of soy sauce and sugar at least 30 minutes. Cut bacon slices in thirds; wrap around water chestnuts and fix with a toothpick. Bake on broiler pan or shallow pan at 350° until bacon is crisp. Makes 30.

Cheddar and Bacon Cracker Spread

1 cup shredded cheddar cheese
1/2 cup margarine
1/4 cup chopped parsley

1/4 cup cooked, crumbled bacon
2 tablespoons sliced green onions

Combine all ingredients in small mixing bowl; beat at medium speed until well mixed, scraping bowl often. Refrigerate 2 hours before serving. Makes 1 1/4 cups.

Magic Finger Jello

2 envelopes unflavored gelatin
1 pkg. (6-ounce) or 2 pkgs. (3-ounce) Jell-O
2 1/2 cups water

Dissolve unflavored gelatins in one cup of cold water. Set aside. In a saucepan, bring 1 cup of water to a boil and add Jell-O. Bring to a boil and remove from heat. Add gelatin mixture. Stir and add 1/2 cup cold water. Pour into a lightly greased pan and set in the refrigerator until solid (about 2 hours). Cut into squares (or use a cookie cutter) and store in an airtight container in the refrigerator.

Luncheons and Brunches

Because afternoon is a popular time to entertain, luncheons and brunches are popular shower ideas. A wide variety of foods is appropriate: egg dishes, casseroles, sandwiches, fruit salads, poultry or seafood salads, and soups.

Be creative, but feel free not to fuss. Remember that, although good food is important, it is not the reason for the party. So, again, prepare as much as you can ahead of time to leave yourself free to enjoy the party.

One easy, fun approach is a salad potluck. Guests bring their favorite salads or chopped salad ingredients: lettuce, tomatoes, green peppers, carrots, celery, sprouts, grated cheese, sliced olives, chicken. You provide a variety of dressings, rolls, beverages, and desserts. Arrange everything on a buffet and allow guests to create their own salads.

Cheese-Onion Pie

1 1/2 cups fine cracker crumbs (about 40 crackers)
1/3 cup butter or margarine, melted
3 cups thinly sliced onions (3 large onions)
2 tablespoons butter

1 cup milk
3 eggs, slightly beaten
1 teaspoon salt
1/4 teaspoon pepper
8 ounces shredded cheddar (about 2 cups)

Combine crumbs and melted butter; press evenly into 9" pie pan. Brown onions in remaining butter; place in crust. Scald milk; add slowly to beaten eggs, stirring constantly. Add salt, pepper, and cheese. Pour mixture over onions. Bake at 350° for 30-40 minutes, until a knife inserted in the center comes out clean. Serves 6-8.

Open-face Turkey Sandwiches

2 cups diced, cooked turkey breast
1 can (8-ounce) unsweetened pineapple chunks, drained
3/4 cup diced celery
3/4 cup chopped apple
1/3 cup mayonnaise

1/4 teaspoon white pepper
1/4 teaspoon curry powder
6 slices bread
2 tablespoons mayonnaise
6 crisp lettuce leaves

Combine first seven ingredients; stir until well mixed. Cover and refrigerate at least 2 hours. Toast bread if desired; spread with remaining mayonnaise; top with lettuce. Spoon turkey mixture evenly on each sandwich. Makes 6 sandwiches.

Pasta Salad

8 ounces tortellini shells
1/4 cup red wine vinegar
1 small onion, chopped

1/4 green pepper, chopped
1 can water chestnuts, drained and sliced

Cook, drain, and cool shells. Combine all ingredients; chill and marinate at least 3 hours before serving.

Chinese Chicken Salad

2 cups cooked chicken or turkey, diced
2 stalks celery, chopped (1 cup)
1 can (8 1/2 ounces) water chestnuts, drained and sliced
2 green onions, thinly sliced
2 canned pimentos, drained and slivered
1 can (10 ounce) bamboo shoots, drained
3/4 cup mayonnaise
2 tablespoons soy sauce
1 tablespoon lemon juice

Combine chicken and vegetables; toss and chill. Stir mayonnaise, soy sauce, and lemon juice together; chill. Combine both mixtures and toss just before serving. Serves 4-6.

Hot Seafood Salad

1 pound crabmeat
2 cans shrimp or 1 pound fresh shrimp
2 cups chopped celery
1 green pepper, chopped
1 can mushrooms, drained
1 can sliced water chestnuts
2 ounces almonds, slivered or sliced
1 medium onion, chopped
1 pint mayonnaise (*not* salad dressing)
2 teaspoons Worcestershire sauce

Mix all ingredients 24 hours before serving. Cover and refrigerate. Top with buttered bread crumbs and bake 30 minutes at 400°. Serves 8-10.

Chicken Broccoli Hotdish

30 ounces broccoli spears, cooked crisp-tender
4 1/2 cups chicken, broken into pieces (4 breasts)
2 cans cream of chicken soup
1 cup mayonnaise
1 teaspoon curry powder mixed in 2 teaspoons butter
1 cup cheddar cheese, grated
3/4 cup buttered bread crumbs or crushed potato chips

Layer broccoli and chicken in greased 9″ × 13″ pan. Mix all other ingredients except crumbs and pour over top. Top with crumbs or chips. Bake at 350° for 30-45 minutes. (Can be assembled the day before and baked just before serving.) Serves 8-10.

Desserts

When you're entertaining in the afternoon or evening, consider a selection of dessert coffees, fancy teas, and liqueurs. Then bring on the cookies, bars, and candies, or throw an all-out chocolate extravaganza. But don't forget those guests who need to avoid calories or caffeine: Include a fresh fruit plate and at least one caffeine-free beverage. Arrange cookies, bars, or small cakes on plastic wedding-cake tiers, if you can.

Poppy Seed Coffee Cake

1 package yellow cake mix
1 package coconut instant pudding mix
4 eggs

1 cup hot water
1/2 cup vegetable oil
1/4 cup poppy seeds

Heat oven to 350°. Grease and flour 10″ tube pan or bundt pan. Combine all ingredients in large mixing bowl; blend. Beat 4 minutes at medium speed. Pour batter into pan. Bake 50 minutes. Serve warm or cold. Serves 12-18.

Sour Cream Coffee Cake

1/2 cup butter or margarine, softened
1/2 cup shortening
1 cup sugar
2 eggs
2 cups all-purpose flour
1 teaspoon soda
1/2 teaspoon salt
1 cup sour cream
1 teaspoon vanilla

Topping
1/2 cup granulated sugar
1/3 cup brown sugar, packed
1 teaspoon cinnamon
1 cup chopped pecans

Heat oven to 350°. Grease 9″ × 13″ pan. Cream butter, shortening, and sugar; beat in eggs. Combine flour, soda, and salt; add alternately to butter mixture with sour cream and vanilla. Pour half of batter into pan. Mix topping ingredients together in small bowl and sprinkle half this mixture over batter in pan. Spoon remaining batter over topping; spread lightly to cover. Sprinkle remaining topping over batter. Bake 30-35 minutes. Serve warm or cold. Serves 12-20.

French Silk Pie

9″ baked pie shell or graham cracker
    crust
3/4 cup butter, softened
1 cup sugar
1 teaspoon vanilla

3 eggs
whipped cream
almonds
3 squares (3 ounces) unsweetened
    chocolate, melted and cooled

Blend butter and sugar in mixing bowl; add vanilla. Add eggs, one at a time, beating well after each. Blend in chocolate. Pour into pie shell. Chill at least one hour before serving. Garnish with whipped cream and almonds. Keep refrigerated.

Pink Lemonade/Ice Cream Pie

3/4 cup gingersnap crumbs
2/3 cup graham cracker crumbs (about 8 crackers)
1 tablespoon sugar

1/4 cup melted butter or margarine
1 quart softened vanilla ice cream
1 can (6 ounces) thawed frozen pink lemonade concentrate

Heat oven to 350°. Combine crumbs, sugar, and butter; press firmly onto bottom and sides of an 8″ or 9″ pie pan. Bake 10 minutes; cool. Combine ice cream and lemonade; mix well. Pour into crust. Freeze until firm. Garnish with thin lemon slices and/or mint leaves. Serve frozen or *slightly* thawed.

Pumpkin Ice Cream Pie

9″ graham cracker crust
1/4 cup brown sugar, packed
3/4 cup canned pumpkin
1/2 teaspoon cinnamon
1/4 teaspoon ginger

dash of nutmeg
dash of cloves
1/4 teaspoon salt
1 quart vanilla ice cream
1/2 cup chopped walnuts

Combine brown sugar, pumpkin, spices, and salt in small saucepan. Boil 30 seconds, stirring constantly. Cool thoroughly. Scoop ice cream into mixing bowl; add cooled pumpkin mixture; blend. (Do not allow ice cream to melt.) Fold in walnuts. Pour into crust; freeze until firm. Garnish with whipped cream and sprinkle with nutmeg, if desired.

Cashew Caramel Yummies

2 eggs, slightly beaten
1/2 cup brown sugar, packed
1/2 cup granulated sugar
1/2 cup chopped, salted cashews
3/4 cup all-purpose flour
1/2 teaspoon baking powder
1/4 teaspoon salt

Topping
2 tablespoons softened butter or margarine
1/4 cup brown sugar, packed
1 1/2 tablespoons cream
1/3 cup salted cashews

Heat oven to 350°. Combine first three ingredients; stir in 1/2 cup cashews. Combine next three ingredients; stir into egg/sugar mixture. Pour into greased, 9″ square pan; bake 20-25 minutes. Combine topping ingredients. Remove pan from oven and spread with topping mixture. Broil 1-3 minutes or until bubbly. Cool, cut into bars. Makes approximately 20-24 bars.

Cinnamon and Sugar Snack Bread

1 loaf frozen white bread dough, thawed
1/2 stick butter or margarine
1/2 cup sugar

1 teaspoon cinnamon, to taste
1/2 cup sliced almonds

Press thawed bread dough into greased 9″ × 13″ pan; allow it to rise several hours. Spread with softened margarine. Combine sugar and cinnamon; sprinkle over top. Sprinkle almonds on top. Bake at 375° for 20-25 minutes or until golden brown. Serve warm. Serves approximately 20.

Filled Chocolate Cupcakes

1 package chocolate cake mix
32 cupcake papers
chopped walnuts
powdered sugar

Filling
8 ounces cream cheese, softened
1 egg plus 1 egg yolk
dash of salt
12 ounces chocolate chips

Mix cake as directed; fill cupcake papers 1/3 full. In a separate bowl, combine filling ingredients; drop a heaping teaspoon of filling on each cupcake. Sprinkle with chopped walnuts and powdered sugar. Bake 20 minutes at 350°. Makes 32 cupcakes.

Beverages

When deciding whether to serve alcohol at your shower, consider the attitudes of the bride, other guests, and yourself. Opinions may vary widely. If you do serve punches that contain alcohol, be sure to label them or tell guests that alcohol is an ingredient. You should also provide a nonalcoholic beverage, particularly if you're not too familiar with some of your guests.

Serving decaffeinated coffee is another good idea. It's easier than serving both kinds and will more likely make a hit with your guests than if you serve only caffeinated.

Frozen Daiquiris

8 cups 7-Up
4 cups light rum
1 can (12 ounces) frozen lemonade
    concentrate, thawed

1 can (12 ounces) frozen limeade
    concentrate, thawed
6 tablespoons powdered sugar
filberts (optional)

Mix first five ingredients in a 1-gallon plastic container. Store in a freezer over-night; it will get slushy but should not freeze. Stir before serving; garnish with filberts, if desired. Makes 30 4-ounce cups. (Can also be made without the rum.)

Wedding Punch

3 large cans frozen orange juice *and* 9
    cans water
3 small cans frozen lemonade *and* 9 cans
    water

1 large can pineapple juice
1 box frozen, crushed strawberries
1 cup sugar
2 quarts ginger ale

Mix all ingredients well; freeze some in mold for punch bowl (see p. 58 to make an ice ring). Add 2 quarts ginger ale when ready to serve. Serves 35.

Serving Suggestions

- When serving large trays of small items on your buffet table, prepare two complete trays of each item. Then, as the first tray on the table becomes depleted, the second complete tray can be brought out from the kitchen to replace it.

- Before pouring hot coffee or cold punch into a serving container, temper it with hot or cold water. Not only will it lessen the chance of breaking a glass pitcher, your beverages will stay hot or cold much longer.

- A basket with a handle makes a convenient and pretty hors d'oeuvres tray to pass from guest to guest. For an extra touch, tie a ribbon on the handle and line it with a ruffled cloth.

- Soups can be as plain or as fancy as you wish; they need not be difficult to serve. Place a tureen on your table with a ladle and mugs or pretty paper "hot cups." Set out a bowl of croutons for garnish.

Special Equipment

You might want to rent or borrow some of the following if you're planning a large affair:

card tables and folding chairs	large serving trays
coffeemaker	pitchers
punch bowl and cups	champagne glasses

Garnishes

A pretty garnish can add a festive touch to any serving tray or punch bowl. Here are a few ideas:

- Float an ice ring in a punch bowl or set it on a platter to keep appetizers cold. To make an ice ring, layer fruits such as cherries or citrus slices and water (or some of your punch) an inch at a time in a ring mold. Freeze each layer before adding the next. By using punch instead of water, you avoid diluting your punch as the ice melts.

- Traditional garnishes are carrot curls, sculpted lemons, radish flowers, tomato roses, and scallion brushes. Try them if you have time!

- Arrange a circle of shiny green lemon leaves around the edge of an hors d'oeuvres platter. Tuck in a few tiny mums and daisies and several small bunches of green grapes here and there.

Other eye-appealing garnishes:

- bright red cherry tomatoes
- bunches of watercress
- shiny olives
- pimento strips
- avocado slices
- lemon, lime, or orange slices

- hard-boiled egg slices
- cucumber slices
- baby dill pickles
- a sprinkling of paprika
- crisp parsley or mint sprigs
- crumbled cooked egg yolk

Chapter
Six

Buying the Gift

Selecting the gift—which is, after all, the major purpose of the party—can be a pleasure or a real headache. It depends on how well you know the tastes and needs of the couple. If you and your guests know them well, selecting a gift is no problem. But if not, help yourself and your guests by asking the bride, groom, or their families about preferred gifts: the items they need most, styles, color choices, sizes. Fill out the wish list included later in this chapter and use it to advise your guests, or enclose copies in your invitations. If your shower has a gift theme (kitchen, bath, or linens, for example), use only the corresponding sections of the wish list.

Another problem in selecting shower gifts is the gifts themselves—many of the things a couple needs are not at all glamorous. Wooden spoons, mops, sheets, and dishcloths often don't seem to merit the attention of a shower. So, either on your own or together with other guests, put together a "theme gift," combining several related items in one package. Wrap each component individually to prolong the gift-opening suspense. Here are a few suggestions:

- Combine a French bread basket with some checkered cloth napkins.

- Fill a pottery jar with assorted kitchen utensils: wooden spoons, spatulas, and whisks, among others.

- Fill a bathroom wastebasket with matching bath accessories, pretty soaps, and coordinated guest towels.

- Fill a brightly colored plastic bucket with an assortment of sponges, polishing cloths, scrub brushes, rubber gloves, and cleaning products. Include a list of your favorite cleaning hints or a book of house-care hints.

- Fill a laundry basket with clothespins, laundry detergent, stain remover, fabric softener, spray starch, and a portable plastic drying rack.

- Dress up a box of basic dish towels or dishcloths by adding a few decorative ones for entertaining.

Be creative. Choose gifts you would like to have yourself or have found useful in the past—the couple probably will, too.

Tip: Ask guests to write a short description of their gifts on the back of the gift card. This will minimize the chance of a mix-up and help the person recording the gifts at the party. (Also see the gift record form in the appendix.)

Practical Gift Suggestions

The following list of suggested gifts is meant to be a guide; it is certainly not all inclusive. And prices will vary, depending on where you shop and the brands you choose.

Under $10

Household Items
Guest towels
Fancy soaps
Kitchen utensils
Napkin rings
Cleaning supplies
Laundry basket
Cake pans, cookie sheets
Candles

Personal Items
Bath oil
Satin lingerie holders
Padded satin hangers
Lacy panties
Pantyhose
Packets of bubble bath
Sachets

$10 to $20

Household items	**Personal items**
Toaster	Slippers
Mixer	Slip
Set of placemats	Camisole
Set of mixing bowls	Bath powder
Cookware	Cologne
Tablecloth	
Casual glassware	
Serving pieces	

Over $20

Many of these items are out of an individual's price range but make excellent group gifts.

Household items	**Personal items**
Blender	Peignoir set
Food processor	Hair dryer
Other small appliances	Makeup mirror
Card table and chairs	Robe
Bathroom hamper	Perfume
Silver	Nightgown
China	Matching bra and panties
Crystal	
Sheets	
Towels	

Handcrafted and Unusual Gifts

It may be tempting to purchase a hand-painted, china picture frame, rather than the shatter-proof casserole listed among the couple's needs. Go ahead, if you know the couple and their tastes well and if they're not lacking the essentials. But if they are eating from paper plates with plastic utensils, they may not appreciate a china napkin holder—unless, of course, it appeals to their need for aesthtics in a time of austerity.

Craft fairs, boutiques, and artists' co-ops are good sources of unique gifts. But before you buy a gift, be certain that the color, size, and style are exactly right—many of these items cannot be returned.

Some popular handcrafted gifts include:

- Fabric-lined baskets

- Hand-painted pottery

- Frames of hand-painted china, brass, silver, or fabric (for photos or to hold the couple's wedding invitation)

- Embroidered linens

- Handmade lace lingerie

- A jigsaw puzzle, made from the couple's engagement photo. (Ads for these can be found in the back pages of many magazines.)

Wish List

Copy the parts of the following wish list that apply to your shower and ask the couple to fill in their preferences. Keep this master list to advise guests, or make copies and enclose them in your invitations. Your guests will be grateful for the guidelines it provides. In the end, each will have chosen just the right gift.

If the bride and groom have registered for gifts at a store, they may have already prepared a detailed wish list. Ask them for a copy to help you put together the wish list. And be sure to mention in the invitation where the couple has registered for certain types of gifts. (Also see the following section on gift registration, p. 68.)

Wish List

Furniture Style _____
Preferred Wood _____
Preferred Metal _____

Bath 1	Colors	_____
	Towel Sizes	_____
	Style	_____
Bath 2	Colors	_____
	Towel Sizes	_____
	Style	_____
Bedroom 1	Colors	_____
	Bedding Size	_____
	Style	_____
Bedroom 2	Colors	_____
	Bedding Size	_____
	Style	_____
Kitchen	Colors	_____
	Style	_____
Dining Room	Colors	_____
	Style	_____
Living Room	Colors	_____
	Style	_____
Other		_____
		_____

The couple is registered at _____

TABLEWARE

Quantity Desired	Quantity Received	Item	Color/Manufacturer/Pattern/Size
		Fine China	
		Serving Pieces (List)	
		Casual China	
		Serving Pieces (List)	
		Fine Stemware (List)	
		Barware	
		Sterling or Silverplate Flatware	
		Stainless Flatware	
		Silver Serving Pieces (List)	
		Table Linens (List)	
		Cookware (List)	

SMALL ELECTRICS

Quantity Desired	Quantity Received	Item	Color/Manufacturer/Pattern/Size
		Toaster	
		Iron	
		Coffeemaker	
		Coffee Grinder	
		Fry Pan	
		Deep Fryer	
		Can Opener	
		Blender Juicer	
		Mixer	
		Waffle Iron	
		Electric Knife	
		Crock Pot	
		Toaster Oven	
		Food Processor	
		Popcorn Popper	
		Microwave Oven	
		Wok	
		Vacuum Cleaner	

OTHER

Quantity Desired	Quantity Received	Item	Color/Manufacturer/Pattern/Size
		Luggage (List)	
		Spice Rack	
		Canister Set	
		Salad Bowls	
		Cutlery	

OTHER cont.

Quantity Desired	Quantity Received	Item	Color/Manufacturer/Pattern/Size
		Bakeware	
		Sheets	
		Pillows	
		Blankets	
		Towels	
		Rugs	
		Bath Accessories	

PERSONAL ITEMS

Color Palette: Spring _____   Summer _____
              Autumn _____   Winter _____

Preferred Colors _____   Preferred Styles _____

_____

Preferred Fragrances _____   Eye Color _____

_____   Hair Color _____

Sizes: Bra _____   Sleepwear _____   Slacks _____   Swimwear _____
        Slip _____   Stockings _____   Dress _____   _____
        Panties _____   Blouse _____   Shoes _____   _____

The bride is registered at _____

Gift Registration

Gift registration services have become incredibly popular. Not only can couples register at department stores for traditional gifts like dishes and silverware, but they can also register at specialty stores featuring gifts like lingerie, houseplants, sporting goods, and even furniture.

Usually, a registry gives the couple a checklist that includes various gift categories. Gifts such as china, crystal, silver, dinnerware, and flatware are listed quite specifically by pattern and quantity desired. Other gifts—like linens and personal items—usually specify at least color, style, and size; if the couple wants to, they can request specific brands or quantities of items, as well. And they can add other items not on the standard checklist.

The gift registry will keep track of what's been bought for the couple *if* the gift givers report their purchases. In fact, some registries update their lists daily. Many registries will also handle over-the-phone orders, which is handy for out-of-town shoppers; gift wrapping and even delivery may be available, for a fee.

Most gift registries recommend that couples sign up about three months before the wedding, which is just in time for showers. So find out where the couple has registered for what types of gifts, and pass this information on to your shower guests. Gift registries are a wonderful service, for both the gift giver and receiver. Be sure to use them when you can.

Gift-wrapping Suggestions

- Department stores charge plenty for their professional gift wrap, which is usually adorned with a useless plastic umbrella or bride. Rather than waste your money, custom-wrap the gift yourself. Purchase pretty paper and ribbon or a ready-made bow; reserve an inexpensive part of your gift to use as a unique decoration on the outside. Then wrap your gift as usual and tie your extra gift to the bow. For instance, if your gift is a set of mixing bowls, tie a ribbon around a set of wooden spoons and fasten it to the package.

- Colorful gift bags are fun, and you can make your own. Wrap paper around a box a little larger than your gift, leaving the end open. Fasten the paper together with clear tape or rubber cement; crease the edges. Slide the box out the open end, and trim the top of the bag with pinking shears. Insert the gift. Punch two holes near the top of the bag; thread a ribbon through and tie it. You can also punch a hole in your gift card and hang it from the ribbon. That way, your card won't get lost or mixed up with one from another gift.

- You can make a beautiful tissue-paper flower to use for a bow. Cut six to eight layers of tissue paper into rectangles, 8 × 5 inches. (You can vary the size to make larger bows, once you master the smaller ones.) Use just one color of tissue or several to match your package. Accordion-fold layers of tissue in one-inch folds, then trim like this:

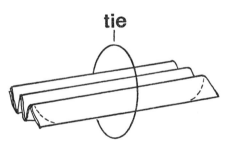

Attach a pipe cleaner around the center of the folded tissue and twist it tightly to cinch the center. Fan out the accordion folds and gently pull the layers of "petals" out to form a flower.

Traditions from Around the World

Chapter Seven

It's fun to learn about the beliefs, customs, and stories concerning marriage that have been passed down through the generations. Here is a sampling. Read some of them at your shower for a sure-fire conversation starter.

Marry in white, you've chosen all right.

Marry in blue, your love is true,

Marry in pearl, you'll live in a whirl,

Marry in brown, you'll live out of town,

Marry in red, you'd be better off dead,

Marry in yellow, ashamed of the fellow,

Marry in green, ashamed to be seen,

Marry in pink, your spirits will sink.

—Origin unknown

Historic Traditions

The Wedding

- The church has been the most common setting for weddings since A.D. 1215, when Pope Innocent III declared it church law.

- The ancients believed that the sun was the great source of fertilizing power, so the summer months, when the sun shone brightly, were felt to be the luckiest months for marriage.

- Ancient Greeks and Romans honored Juno, the goddess of love and marriage, with festivals and celebrations in June. As a result, June brides expected happiness and prosperity.

Some early American customs concerned both the day and the time of the wedding.

- Some believed the wedding ceremony should be completed between the half hour and the hour. The rising hand of the clock was said to denote success and rising fortune. Weddings performed after the hour, when the hand was falling, meant marriages plagued by bad luck.

- Another belief held that weddings should be scheduled when the moon was almost full or on the increase.

- In the 17th century, morning weddings were not recommended. It was thought the bridegroom was apt to be unshaven and dirty—the result of either early morning chores in the country or a last round of all-night bachelor parties in the city.

Rings

- The engagement tradition was born when Pope Innocent III decreed in A.D. 1215 that a waiting period be observed between betrothal and marriage. This led to the tradition of two rings. The engagement ring, first known as the betrothal ring, was originally given as partial payment for the bride (a symbol of the groom's good intentions).

- Diamonds were first used in engagement rings in medieval Italy. Their durability symbolized enduring love.

- In ancient Egypt, the circular shape of the wedding ring meant unending love and commitment. The rings were originally made of rushes or hemp and were replaced yearly.

- Engagement and wedding rings are worn on the third finger of the left hand because the early Egyptians believed the vein of that finger ran directly to the heart.

- The medieval groom placed the ring on three of the bride's fingers, symbolizing the Trinity. Together, the couple recited, "In the name of the Father, the Son, and the Holy Ghost. Amen," while moving the ring from one finger to the next. By the "Amen," the ring was finally in position on the third finger of the left hand.

- The traditional Greek bride wears her ring on her left hand until her wedding, when it is moved to her right hand.

The Trousseau

- The word *trousseau* comes from the French word *trousse*, meaning "bundle." It originally described the bundle of clothing and personal possessions the bride carried with her to her new home; later, it was used to refer to her dowry.

The Veil

- The bridal veil originated in ancient Greece and Rome, where it symbolized youth and virginity. The custom persists in some Middle Eastern countries, where the groom never sees his bride unveiled until after the wedding.

- Ancient Greek and Roman veils were flame red; early Christians chose white or purple.

- Nellie Custis may have made the lace veil fasionable. She wore a long lace scarf to marry Major Lawrence Lewis, President Washington's aide, because of flattering comments he made after seeing her face through a lace curtain.

The Wedding Dress

- Until the 19th century, a bride rarely bought a special dress for her wedding. She wore here best dress—possibly a family heirloom or a national costume. White became the favored color when Anne of Brittany married Louis XII in white; it was thought to symbolize purity and to ward off evil.

- Wearing a green dress has been taboo everywhere but in Norway. It was believed that green symbolized jealousy—or perhaps hid grass stains that hinted of illicit romps in the meadow!

The Garter

- In 14th century France, the wedding guests rushed for the bride's garter (which symbolized the release of the virgin girdle), because it bestowed great luck. But because people were hurt in the onslaught, brides began to remove their garters and throw them instead.

"Something Old, Something New . . ."

It became a tradition in Britain for a bride to wear these things in her wedding:

- The "something old" must be something that has belonged to a happily married woman to ensure the transfer of happiness to the bride.

- The "something new" is usually the wedding gown or shoes.

- The "something borrowed" should be an object made of gold to guarantee future wealth and fortune.

- The "something blue," taken from a custom of ancient Israel, symbolizes fidelity, modesty, and love.

- The new penny (or sixpence) should be worn in the heel of the left shoe, where it assures the bride a wealthy and prosperous future.

Bouquets and Flowers

- The bridal bouquet originated with the ancient Romans. It was their custom to light the first lamp in a couple's new home with a torch and then toss the torch to the wedding party. In the 14th century, the French substituted a bouquet for the torch and added that whoever caught the bouquet would be wed next.

- Early Roman brides carried bouquets of garlic, chives, and other strong herbs to symbolize fertility and to drive away evil spirits. Later, small stalks of sheat or corn stalks and leaves, which symbolized fruitfulness, were also carried. The bride sometimes wore laurel leaves in her hair as a sign of victory.

- The Saracens chose orange blossoms for a wedding flower. Because the orange tree blooms and bears fruit at the same time, it was thought to contain youth, purity, and fertility in one bud. The Crusaders may have brought this custom to the West.

- Myrtle in a wedding bouquet brings good luck; apple blossoms, better things to come; ivy assures both good luck and eternal fidelity; lilies signify purity.

- In the late 1800s, an American bride sometimes carried as many small bouquets as she had bridesmaids. The bouquets were tied together, one of them concealing a ring. When the bride and groom were ready to leave, the room was darkened, and the bride threw the bouquets to the guests. Whoever caught the bouquet with the ring inside was thought next to be married. The bride and groom then exited secretly.

The Bridal Party

The bridal party has had many different duties over the years.

- At one time, the groom and his attendants went to the home of the bride to claim her. They were not permitted to enter until they gave some form of gift to the maids who protected the bride.

- The early Roman wedding party, in addition to participating in the ceremony, guarded the couple's money and belongings during the festivities.

- Traditionally, bridesmaids and ushers dressed like the bride and groom to confuse evil spirits.

- One superstition holds that it is unlucky for at least one groomsman and one bridesmaid to be happily married.

- If an unmarried bridesmaid wishes to marry soon, she should carry a piece of wedding cake in her pocket until the honeymoon is over. If a woman has been a bridesmaid three times and still isn't married, the fable says she never will.

Reception

The wedding reception, a tradition found in most cultures, can be as staid as cake and punch in the church basement or as wild as the Norwegian custom of dancing and reveling all night long.

- The custom of toasting the newly wedded couple is believed to have originated in 16th century France, where lavish feasts were popular. A man drank to the health of the bride, and then placed a piece of bread at the bottom of the wine goblet and passed the cup to each guest. The bride, last to receive the cup, ate the wine-soaked toast and received everyone's best wishes.

- The custom of the bride and groom having the first dance alone may have evolved from puritanical European tradition. The couple was expected to dance the first three dances together, while the wedding guests observed them closely to determine if any premarital lovemaking had taken place.

The Wedding Cake

- The wedding cake has been a part of the wedding celebration since the early Romans broke a thin loaf over the bride's head at the end of the ceremony. The wheat from which the loaf was made symbolized fertility. The crumbs that fell were eagerly snatched and eaten by the wedding guests, who believed them to bring good luck.

- In medieval England, each guest brought a bun or small cake to the wedding. These sweets were piled atop each other, and the bride and groom kissed over the stack to ensure many healthy children. The modern, tiered wedding cake was born when a baker amassed all the cakes together and covered them with frosting.

- One supersitition holds that if the bride tastes her wedding cake before the wedding, she will forfeit her husband's love. But if she keeps a piece of the cake, she is assured of his lifelong fidelity.

- Another custom holds that, after the first wedding in a family, part of the cake must be kept in the house until all the daughters are wed, lest they become old maids.

Wheat and Rice

- The custom of throwing rice at departing newlyweds comes from the Orient, where the rice symbolizes fertility and means "May you always have a full pantry."

- Ancient Greeks and Romans tossed kernels of wheat and corn at the new couple to wish them luck and prosperity.

Shoes
- Tying old shoes to the back of the newlyweds' car comes from Hebraic history. The groom and the bride's father exchanged shoes at the wedding to symbolize her transfer to the new home.

- In Anglo-Saxon marriages, the bride's father demonstrated the transfer of authority by taking a shoe from his daughter's foot and handing it to his new son-in-law. Upon receiving the shoe, the groom became the bride's new master; he held the shoe up and lightly tapped the head of the bride three times to demonstrate his new authority.

The Threshold
- Ancient Romans believed the goddess Vesta, ruler of hearth and threshold, was connected with virgins. It was considered bad luck for a new bride to stumble or trip as she entered her new home, so her husband carried her over the threshold.

The Honeymoon
- In early "marriages by capture," the idea of the honeymoon began when the groom kept his bride hidden to prevent searching relatives from finding her.

- Ancient Teutons celebrated weddings with great feasting and drinking. They brewed a special wine from honey and yeast, and consumed it for thirty days—from one full moon, under which the couple was married, to the next. The word *honeymoon* was coined from this custom, and the word *bridal* derives from the name of the drink, *brydealo* or *brideale*.

- It is still considered good luck for a bride to take something borrowed with her on her honeymoon as a link to her past life.

- An American custom recommends the following recipe: "Take a pound of Limburger cheese and spread it between two towels to make a poultice. Place it under the pillow of the newlyweds on their first night together and good fortune and prosperity will always be theirs."

- Years ago, on the morning after the wedding (assuming the evening before had been successful), it was customary for the bride to ask the groom for the "morning's gift." The bride could ask for any sum of money or piece of property she wanted, and the groom was honor-bound to give it to her. If he could not afford her request, he had to make another offer. The "morning's gift" had to be fulfilled soon after and became the basis for the wife's economic independence. The rule of thumb: The better the wedding night, the bigger the gift.

Superstitions about Children and Fertility

- If a woman holds a newborn on her first visit to see the baby, she will become a mother.

- If a married woman is the first to see a recently born infant, she will have the next child.

- The woman who lays her coat or hat on a stranger's bed will have a baby.

- If you go swimming the first day you are married, you will have twins.

- Count the seeds in an apple to discover how many children you'll have.

- Count the number of veins branching out from the main vein in your wrist to see how many children you'll have.

- A poor man is certain to have many children.

- A happily married couple will have beautiful children. If they quarrel continually, their children will be ugly.

National Customs

Africa

- Some tribes still bind the bride's and groom's wrists together with braided grass during the wedding ceremony.

- In Algeria, the bridegroom throws eggs at his bride during their marriage consummation. The pelting ensures her fertility and easy childbirth.

- Among the Bantu Kavironda tribes, the bride and groom must consummate their marriage before a large group of young girls and women. This is to show publicly that the marriage is legal—it is believed the women will spread the word more quickly than men. The husband's prowess and virility, along with the success of the consummation, are measured by the amount of giggling and embarrassment the witnesses express.

Belgium
- Many years ago, a Belgian bride stitched her name on her wedding handkerchief, then framed it after the wedding, and displayed it until the next woman in her family married.

Bermuda
- Wedding cakes in Bermuda are topped with a tiny tree sapling. At the reception, the newlyweds plant the tree.

Britain
- Because it was considered a lucky color, British brides and grooms rode in gray carriages (now, automobiles) in the wedding procession.

- In small villages, the bride and her wedding party would walk to the church together. A small girl led the procession, dropping flower blossoms on the road so the bride's path through life would always be happy and flower laden.

- Musicians often led the wedding procession and bridesmaids and flower girls carried sheaves of wheat, symbolizing fertility.

- In Somerset county, the wedding party is locked in the churchyard and released only upon payment of a handful of coins.

- In Guernsey, newlyweds traditionally placed a coin on the head of a prehistoric stone figure in the churchyard for luck.

- A British bride carries a lump of sugar in her bodice to assure sweetness all her married life.

- It is considered good luck to see a wolf, spider, or toad on the way to the wedding. But it is bad luck to meet a friar, priest, dog, cat, hare, lizard, or snake.

China
- Red, the color for love and joy in Old China, was once the favored choice for the bride's dress, candles, gift boxes, and money envelopes.

- It was believed that the groom would rule the bride if he was able to sit on part of the bride's dress when they seated themselves on the bed on their wedding night.

- In Canton, three long strips of red paper were suspended from the canopy of the nuptial bed to extend good wishes to the couple.

Czechoslovakia

- Rural brides wear rosemary wreaths woven for them on the eve of their weddings.

Eskimos

- On the wedding night, it is customary for the bridesmaids and the bride to warm the bed for the groom. He may decide how many of the bridesmaids will remain in the bed during the marriage consummation. But if the groom dallies with any of the bridesmaids during the night, the bride may hit him with a moccasin or a slab of blubber.

Finland

- Long ago, Finnish brides wore golden crowns. After the wedding, the bride was blindfolded. As the unmarried women danced around the bride, the guests sang, "It has been, it has gone, never will the bride dance with the crown again." The bride then reached out and placed the crown on one girl's head. This girl was next to marry.

France

- Many couples carry on the old tradition of drinking the reception toast from an engraved two-handled cup, the *coup de mariage*, which they pass on to future generations.

- An old peasant custom required the bride's father to lay a long loaf of bread in the marriage bed to ensure the bride's fertility and the groom's virility. The condition of the bread the next morning signified the success or failure of the wedding night.

Germany

- In old Germany, a few weeks before the wedding, the couple asked a male friend to be the "inviter." Dressed in his best clothes and carrying a walking stick decorated with ribbons and flowers, he knocked on doors with the stick and invited the guests. Traditionally, he was invited in and given a drink.

- While the groom and his buddies have a stag party, the bride and her friends hold a *polterabend* in front of her house. They smash cups and dishes against her front door, and the bride must sweep up the debris. The noise of the crashing crockery is said to frighten away evil spirits, and the sweeping up brings luck to the newlyweds.

- During the ceremony, it is traditional for the bride and groom to hold candles trimmed with flowers and ribbons.

- Many years ago, when the newly married couple returned to their new home for the reception, a beer stein was thrown over the roof to keep the groom from drinking too much. He then carried his bride over the threshold, and they shared a small piece of bread to ensure they would always have enough to eat.

- It was once believed that if the groom knelt on the hem of the bride's dress at the altar, he would dominate her. She could counter, however, by standing on his foot when they rose again.

- It was customary for the husband to consummate the marriage wearing his socks to avert disease and evil spirits from his wife's bed. It was also expected that he take a lengthy foot bath before the ceremony.

Greece

- A Greek bride carries a lump of sugar in her glove to ensure sweetness all her married life.

Holland

- Dutch families threw a party for the engaged couple before the wedding. The bride and groom sat on thrones under a canopy of evergreens to symbolize everlasting love. One by one, the guests offered their good wishes.

India

- Indian brides dress in vibrant colors, while the groom wears white.

- At the end of the wedding ceremony, the groom's brother sprinkles flower petals on the bridal couple.

- Long ago, a coconut was passed over the bride and groom three times and then shattered on the ground to drive away demons.

- In one region of India where marriages are still arranged, parents of daughters who have no chance to marry a wealthy man "marry" her to a bunch of flowers. They throw the flowers down a well and the daughter becomes a widow. Her parents can then accept the nominal brideprice normally offered widows, and still save face.

Iran (formerly Persia)

- Persian brides believed that, if they added rosewater to the groom's food or drink, their husbands would be bound to them forever.

Ireland

- The traditional Irish wedding cake is a heavy, rich fruitcake made with golden raisins, ground almonds, cherries, and spice.

- An old custom had a bridesmaid hurry to the honeymoon site before the bride and groom arrived. She poured a glass of beer and handed it to the groom after he had carried the bride over the threshold. The groom then "chugged" the beer, tossing the empty glass behind him. If the glass broke, the evening would be a success.

Italy

- For centuries, wedding guests in Italy have tossed *confetti* (sugared almonds) at the newlyweds to wish them happiness.

Japan

- At the wedding feast, Japanese couples drink nine sips of sake (rice wine) from a little, double-spouted kettle, decorated with butterflies. After the first sip, the bride and groom are husband and wife. The kettle signifies that they will share everything; this sharing will help bless their future with children.

Jewish Cultures

- Formerly, it was common to plant a cedar for a newborn boy and a pine for a girl. When the children grew up and married, their respective trees were cut down and used to construct a *huppah* or bridal bower.

- It was once the preferred tradition to hold the ceremony under a starlit sky. The wedding took place under the *huppah* as a reminder of God's promise to Abraham that his descendants would be as numerous as the stars.

- In small European villages, a procession of wedding guests (usually the entire community) carried candles as a sign of rejoicing. The procession wound its way to the village square, where the *huppah* was set up.

- During the Jewish ceremony, the groom smashes a wine glass under his heel as a reminder of the seriousness and fragility of life.

- An Orthodox custom requires the bride, escorted by the two mothers (who carry lit candles), to circle the groom one, three, or seven times under the *huppah* before taking her place at his right side.

- Jewish couples sometimes sign an elaborate *ketubah*, or marriage contract, with the husband's promises to his wife, which is later hung prominently in their home.

Malaysia

- A Malay wedding takes several days. On the first two nights, the bride sits in state with her groom, leaving periodically to change her costume. She may wear as many as twenty different outfits, some from her trousseau and others provided by the *mak andam*. The *mak andam* helps the bride dress, fix her hair, and apply her makeup. She lends her jewelry and furnishes the bedspread for the nuptial bed and the dais upon which the couple sits. She also provides moral support.

Palestine

- Salt, believed to be a preventative, was tossed over the heads of all members of the wedding party before the festivities began.

Peru

- The wedding party decorates the honeymoon bed with red and green chili peppers to assure the bridal couple a fruitful and passionate marriage.

Poland

- Long ago, it was customary for the bride to send a surrogate (usually a sister or close cousin, disguised as the bride) to her wedding ceremony. The groom did likewise. The surrogate couple performed the wedding ceremony and consummation. If no evil came to them within a fortnight, the real bride then performed the wedding rites with the groom.

Rumania

- In Rumania, guests toss sweets and nuts at the newlyweds to wish them prosperity.

Russia

- Both the bride and groom in a Russian Orthodox wedding stand under crowns held by their attendants. The priest gives the couple three drinks of ceremonial wine from the same cup, symbolizing their willingness to drink from the same cup of experience.

Scandinavia

- Eighteenth century Scandinavians believed that chimney sweeps were the bearers of good luck. (People found that once the chimney sweep had finished his work, the incidence of house fires decreased greatly.) If a chimney sweep gave the bride a kiss at her wedding, it was considered the best of luck.

- Until recently, Icelandic brides wore black velvet wedding dresses embroidered with silver and gold.

- An old Scandinavian custom required the bride to be married and to walk to her honeymoon chamber with her shoes untied. She consummated the marriage and slept with the shoes dangling on her feet. It was hoped the shoes would fall off by themselves during the night's activities, so that she would "bear children as easily as she removes her shoes."

- In Norway and Iceland, it was believed that a wedding that took place during a blizzard would be blessed, because the storms of life would already be over for the newlyweds.

- To frighten away trolls (imaginary beasts once thought to bring misfortune), Swedish brides carried bouquets of pungent herbs, and grooms sewed thyme into their clothes.

- Many years ago in Sweden, it was believed that if a small boy slept on the bride's side of the bed on the wedding night, her firstborn would be male.

Scotland

- December 31 is the most popular wedding day in Scotland. On that day, the whole world celebrates with the couple, and by the following morning, they have supposedly been happily married for a year.

- The piper at a Scottish wedding keeps a piece of the bride's garter tied around his pipes.

Serbia

- After a Serbian wedding, at midnight, the head of the groom's family ushered the bride into the groom's room, where he was already undressed and in bed. The father of the groom then bolted the door of the bridal chamber, guzzled a glass of wine, and shattered the empty glass against the door. The wedding party cheered the breakage, which symbolized the imminent loss of the bride's virginity. While the bride and groom remained alone together in their quarters, the guests continued to throw glasses, pots, and other objects at a burlap sack, which was placed against the wedding chamber door. The sack held an egg; when the egg broke, the marriage was officially consummated.

Spain
- At a Spanish wedding, the flower girl (called *la portora de anillos*) dresses exactly like the bride.

Lanka (formerly Ceylon)
- During the wedding and at all ceremonial occasions, a Kandyan groom feeds his bride rice milk cake, which symbolizes good fortune.

Switzerland
- The junior bridesmaid at a Swiss wedding leads the procession to the reception carrying a handful of colored handkerchiefs. Guests may buy one by contributing a few coins to the newlyweds' nest egg.

Thailand
- A marriage in Thailand is performed by either a parent of the bride or groom or by a highly respected friend of one or both families. The ceremony takes place in the bride's home, in the presence of family and attendants. The couple is blessed and advised about the proper conduct for a married couple. During the ceremony, the bride and groom wear a "brahman rope" tied around both their heads like headbands, connected in the middle. It symbolizes the marriage bond and is believed to bring them happiness and wealth.

United States
- In early America, it was believed that if a man married a widow while she was naked (or barefoot and wearing only a shift or smock), he could not be held responsible for any debts she had incurred before their marriage.

- It was once believed that the weather on the wedding day could foretell the pattern of the bride's future. For example, a beautiful morning and a stormy afternoon meant a good beginning but trouble later. The weather on the day after the wedding foretold the groom's life, and the day after that indicated the pattern of their lives together.

- It is good luck if a ray of sunshine falls on the bride when she leaves the church.

- A bride will get a dollar for every flake of snow that falls on her on her wedding day.

- Early American brides sometimes bought a pin from a bridesmaid as soon as they reached the church door from the altar. It was believed that whoever made the first purchase after the ceremony would "rule the nest."

- The chivaree was a popular custom during the 18th and 19th centuries. A group of friends and wedding guests followed the newlyweds to the site of their wedding night to serenade them. However, if the guests were drunk, they were apt to become irreverent and rowdy and generally make fools of themselves.

- Americans have held many supersititions that foretold an impending wedding, including:

  - A chicken coming into the house with a piece of straw in its beak and laying it down

  - A cow lowing during the night

  - A mockingbird flying over or a white dove coming near a house

- Still other superstitions foretold marital happiness:

  - If a cat sneezed in front of a bride the day before her wedding, it was a sign of good luck.

  - A bride could ensure a happy wedding day if she fed a cat out of an old shoe.

  - The events of the trip to the wedding ceremony held significance in early America. To see a lamb or a flock of white birds was good luck; a pig crossing the path of the carriage or a flock of black birds flying overhead did not bode well for the couple.

  - An American bride could ensure good luck by carrying bread in her pockets. When she threw the bread away, she threw away her troubles, as well.

- By giving the minister an odd sum of money as payment for his services, the groom could bring good luck to his marriage.

- A spider crawling on the bride's wedding dress was considered a sign of good fortune.

- A bride must have her hair dressed and her veil put on by a happily married woman for good luck.

- If a bride carried or wore a bit of salt in her glove, shoe, or pocket, she would always be happy. Salt has two virtues: It is hated by witches and devils, and because it is a preservative, it symbolizes lasting friendship and loyalty.

- A bride who sheds tears on her wedding day will always be happy, for she has wept them all away, and after that day, there remains only happiness.

- If the youngest daughter in a family marries before her older sisters, they must dance barefoot or in green stockings at her wedding to bring themselves husbands. To doubly ensure their success, the older sisters should also dance in a pig's trough.

- When she takes her wedding dress off, the bride should throw a stocking over her left shoulder. If it lies in a straight line on the floor, her luck will be continuous. Otherwise, it will be varied and changeable.

- The bride and groom who sleep with their heads to the north on their wedding night will always be happy.

- At a bridal shower, the guest whose gift is the seventh to be opened will be the next to be married.

Wales

- In Wales, a bridesmaid planted a sprig from the bride's bouquet on either side of the couple's front door when she returned from the church. If the plants lived, another wedding would occur when the bush bloomed. If not, the bridesmaid would become an old maid.

Appendix

How to Make Invitations

All of the cards in the Appendix are designed to fit into 4-1/2″ × 5-1/2″ envelopes, which are available at most stationery and department stores. Many shops have color-coordinated envelopes and paper, so you can make the invitations out of pink paper and match them with blue envelopes or use a color scheme that fits the theme you have chosen for the party.

The designs in this book can be photocopied onto your own paper, depending on the type of copying machine available to you, or they can be traced.

Remember: When creating your own invitations, be sure to include all of the pertinent information:

- name(s) of the guest(s) of honor

- the date, time, and address of the shower

- your name, address, and telephone number

- whether or not you want regrets only or RSVP's

- whether the party is for women only or for couples and men

Also include any special directions your guests need to know: food to bring, type of gift, or how to get to the shower.

Single-sided Notes

Below are directions for making single-sided note cards with designs on the front and information inside or on the back of the card. For single-sided cards with shower information on the front, use the back of the card as the mailing side, filling in your address and the guests' mailing addresses. You will save the expense of purchasing envelopes, but use heavy stock paper, so the invitations don't get damaged in the mail.

ON FRONT →

WRITE INFO ON BACK

Folded Notes

Following the directions below, trace or copy your chosen card design on one quarter of a 8-1/2″ × 11″ piece of paper. Then fill in the shower information on the quarter across from it (see diagram). When you fold the paper, you'll have a card with a design on the front and the information inside.

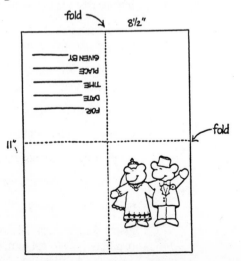

fold ↘ 8½″

GIVEN BY
PLACE
TIME
DATE
FOR

11″

fold

Patchwork

Cut a rectangle of printed paper or calico fabric with a pinking shears; mount on the front of the card. Write your information on the back or inside.

Lingerie

Using the pattern for folded notes, cut the shape of a stocking or other recognizable piece of lingerie from the front panel. Attach a piece of lace to the *underside* of the panel, so the lace shows through the cutout. (Black lace on pink paper is very attractive.) Write your information on the inside.

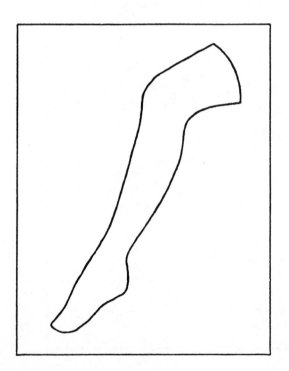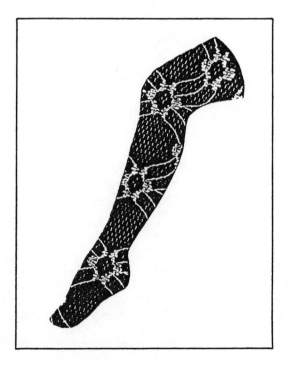

Lace

Cut a piece of lace approximately 1/2″ longer than your folded note. Lay the lace on top of the invitation; fold it where it overlaps and secure on the back with a strip of tape. You'll have an invitation with an extra layer of lace on the top.

Telephone

Cut a phone shape from a piece of black paper; draw in details with chalk, white crayon, or special metallic ink pens. Mount the phone on the front of your card or folded note.

Mop and Pail

Photocopy or trace this design on the front of your card or folded note.

Basket of Good Wishes

Photocopy or trace this design on the front of your card or folded note.

Mystery Box

Photocopy or trace this design on the front of your card or folded note.

Four Seasons

Photocopy or trace this design on the front of your card or folded note.

Bride and Groom

Photocopy or trace this design on the front of your card or folded note.

Hearts and Flowers

Photocopy or trace this design on the front of your card or folded note.

House

Photocopy or trace this design on the front and back of your folded note; fold on the crease and cut the top to conform to the roofline.

Office Memo

Copy this telephone message-slip invitation for an office shower. Be sure to use paper that looks somewhat different than the telephone message slips your company uses, or people might mistake it for a real telephone message and overlook the invitation!

```
┌─────────────────────────────────────────────┐
│ To _____  │
│ Subject _____  │
│                                              │
│           IT'S A PARTY!                      │
│                                              │
│ For _____  │
│ of _____ Department │
│ at _____  │
│ _____  │
│                                              │
│ Date _____    Time _____    │
│ ┌──────────────────┬─────────────────────┐   │
│ │ RSVP             │ Regrets only        │ │ │
│ └──────────────────┴─────────────────────┘   │
│                                              │
│ Message _____  │
│ _____  │
│ _____  │
│ _____  │
│                                              │
│ Contact _____  │
│                                              │
│ Extension _____  │
└─────────────────────────────────────────────┘
```

The Firstborn Profile

As each guest arrives, choose a category below and ask him or her to name a color, number, or the like to fill in the blank. (Don't let guests know what their suggestions are being used for.) If you have more guests than categories, make up a few of your own and add them to the form.

Baby Profile   Date of party _____

First name _____

Middle name _____

hair _____

height _____

eyes _____

weight _____

male _____

female _____

occupation

_____   favorite foods

_____   _____

_____   _____

hobbies   _____

_____   _____

_____   _____

Cartoons

Copy these captionless cartoons and post them at the party; display them together or scatter them around. Provide pens or pencils with the cartoons and invite your guests to write their own captions. At the end of the party, collect the cartoons.

Keepsake Scrapbook

Reproduce this form and use it to record the advice guests offer to the bride and groom. It'll make a nice memento of the shower for the couple to look back on.

Shower Date _____ Shower Given by _____

At this shower we received words of wisdom about: _____

Guest	Advice

Lovegram

Use this form with the activity on p. 39.

Date: _____

To: _____

From: _____

Shower Gift Record

Someone always has to keep track of the shower gifts: who gave what to the bride and groom? Using this form as a record will make the job much easier. It will also provide a nice reminder of the shower, as well as help the couple in preparing thank-yous.

Shower Date _____ Shower Given by _____

Guest   Advice

Anniversaries

Use this list of anniversary gift categories in planning a shower theme or anniversary-related activities.

1 - Paper
2 - Cotton
3 - Leather
4 - Books, fruit, or flowers
5 - Wood or clocks
6 - Iron or candy
7 - Copper, bronze, brass, or wool
8 - Electrical appliances
9 - Pottery or willow
10 - Tin or aluminum
11 - Steel
12 - Silk or linen
13 - Lace
14 - Ivory
15 - Crystal
20 - China
25 - Silver
30 - Pearl
35 - Jade or coral
40 - Ruby
45 - Sapphire
50 - Gold
55 - Emerald
60 - Diamond
75 - Diamond

Trivia Game

Play this game to get all of the guests at the shower involved and talking. You can divide the group into teams and take turns asking questions, or ask questions of the group at large. Each group or individual who answers a question correctly gets a point. Or make up your own similar rules.

Famous Couples Trivia

1 What was the maiden name of Prince Charles' wife?
Answer: Lady Diana Spencer

2 What was the maiden name of Prince Andrew's wife?
Answer: Lady Sarah Ferguson

3 How many times has Elizabeth Taylor been married?
Answer: Seven

4 To whom was she married and divorced twice?
Answer: Richard Burton

5 What two actors from the TV series "Mission: Impossible" were married to each other?
Answer: Barbara Bain and Martin Landau

6 What "hippie" couple of the 1970s was actually married on "The Tonight Show"?
Answer: Tiny Tim and Miss Vicky

7 Who is Popeye's girlfriend
Answer: Olive Oyl

8 What old-time movie couple is probably the most famous dance pair of all time?
Answer: Fred Astaire and Ginger Rogers

9 For whom did King Edward VIII of England abdicate his throne in 1936?
Answer: Wallis Warfield Simpson

10 Name three of Henry VIII's six wives:
Answer: Catherine of Aragon, Anne Boleyn, Jane Seymour, Anne of Cleves, Catherine Howard, Catherine Parr

11 Who was the schoolmarm companion of the Sundance Kid?
Answer: Etta Place

12 How many times has Johnny Carson been married?
Answer: Three

13 What famous model and rock singer were married on a boat cruising around Manhattan?
Answer: Christie Brinkley and Billy Joel

14 What all-American TV series of the fifties and sixties featured a bandleader, his wife, and their two children?
Answer: "The Adventures of Ozzie and Harriet"

15 What popular contemporary comedy team is also a married couple?
Answer: Jerry Stiller and Anne Meara

16 Name two popular comedy teams from the fifties and before who were a married couple, both on TV and in real life.
Answer: George Burns and Gracie Allen and Lucille Ball and Desi Arnaz

17 Name one of the movies in which Paul Newman and Joanne Woodward appeared together.
Answer: "The Long, Hot Summer," "Rally Round the Flag, Boys," "From the Terrace," "Paris Blues," "A New Kind of Love," "Winning," "WUSA," "The Drowning Pool," "Harry and Son"

18 Who sent John Alden to propose to Priscilla Mullins for him?
Answer: Miles Standish

19 What was her reply?
Answer: "Speak for yourself, John."

20 What was the name of Pecos Bill's wife?
Answer: Slue-Foot Sue

21 How many times was Marilyn Monroe married?
Answer: Three

22 Name her husbands.
Answer: James Dougherty, Joe DiMaggio, Arthur Miller

23 Who was William Shakespeare's wife?
Answer: Anne Hathaway

24 Who is Dudley Do-Right's girlfriend?
Answer: Miss Nell

25 Who married Daisy Mae and Li'l Abner?
Answer: Marryin' Sam

26 What is the name of the Dogpatch holiday where the girls chase after the available men to catch a husband?
Answer: Sadie Hawkins Day

27 In the "Nancy" comics, who is Nancy's boyfriend?
Answer: Sluggo

28 Who is Porky Pig's girlfriend?
Answer: Petunia

29 Name the two couples who were neighbors and friends on "The Flintstones."
Answer: Fred and Wilma Flintstone and Barney and Betty Rubble

30 Although she never married him, with whom was Scarlet O'Hara really in love?
Answer: Ashley Wilkes

31 What actress was the big love of Clark Gable's life?
Answer: Carole Lombard

32 What actor was Katherine Hepburn's lifelong love, although she never married him?
Answer: Spencer Tracy

33 Who was Ronald Reagan's first wife?
Answer: Jane Wyman

34 Who were the married couple/crime-solving team in the "Thin Man" series?
Answer: Nick and Nora Charles

35 On the original "I Love Lucy," who were the Ricardos' best friends and neighbors?
Answer: Fred and Ethel Mertz

36 What were Romeo and Juliet's last names?
Answer: Montague and Capulet

37 Who was Adolf Hitler's wife?
Answer: Eva Braun

38 How long were they married?
Answer: Two days.

39 What popular actress married a member of the "Chicago Seven" activists?
Answer: Jane Fonda (to Tom Hayden)

40 Who played "MacMillan and Wife" on TV?
Answer: Rock Hudson and Susan Saint James

Complete the Proverb

Read the first part of each of the following proverbs and see who can complete it correctly.

1. What God hath joined, . . .

Answer.   . . . let no man put asunder.

2. Marry the man today . . .

Answer.   . . . and change his ways tomorrow.

3. It's just as easy to marry . . .

Answer.   . . . a rich man as a poor one.

4. The course of true love . . .

Answer.   . . . never runs smooth.

5. Why buy a cow . . .

Answer.   . . . when you can get the milk for free?

6. Lucky in cards, . . .

Answer.   . . . unlucky in love.

7. Marriages are made . . .

Answer.   . . . in heaven.

8. It is better to have loved and lost . . .

Answer.   . . . than to never have loved at all

9. Never marry for money: . . .

Answer.   . . . you can borrow it cheaper.

10. All is fair . . .

Answer.   . . . in love and war.

11. A good wife makes . . .

Answer.   . . . a good husband.

12. Love it . . .

Answer.   . . . or leave it.

13. Marry in haste, . . .

Answer.   . . . repent at leisure.

14. Love is lost . . .

Answer.   . . . if not given away.

15. You can't catch a man . . .

Answer.   . . . with a gun.

16. She who marries for money, . . .

Answer.   . . . earns it.

17. There's only one good mother-in-law, . . .

Answer.   . . . and she is dead.

18. A deaf husband and a blind wife . . .

Answer.   . . . are always a happy couple.

19. Love is blind, . . .

Answer.   . . . but the neighbors ain't.

20. Love means never . . .

Answer.   . . . having to say you're sorry.

The Best Baby Shower Book
by Courtney Cooke

Who says baby showers have to be dull? Finally, a contemporary guide for planning baby showers that's chock-full of helpful hints, recipes, decorating ideas, and activities that are fun without being juvenile.

Order #1239

The Best Party Book
by Penny Warner

Over 1,000 tips and ideas for fun and successful parties for any occasion. Whether it's a birthday, anniversary, reunion, holiday, retirement, or the Super Bowl, this creative guide shows even the most inexperienced host how to throw a great party.

Order #6089

The Best Bridal Shower Party Game Book
by Courtney Cooke

Complete with tear-out duplicate game sheets for shower guests, the eight entertaining games and activities in this book will "break the ice" and get the celebration off to a fast and funny start.

Order #6060

The Best Couple's Shower Party Game Book
by Courtney Cooke

This unique couple's shower party game book contains eight entertaining games and activities that will "break the ice" and get the celebration off to a fast and funny start.

Order #6061

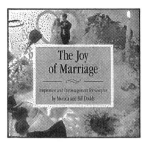

The Joy of Marriage
by Monica and Bill Dodds

A gift of love for married couples. With clever one-line messages, it accentuates the everyday romantic, caring, and playful elements of married life. Filled with beautiful, touching photographs.

Order #3504

For Better And For Worse
The Best Quotes about Marriage
Selected by Bruce Lansky

This collection of marriage wit and wisdom is an ideal gift for wedding showers, bachelor/bachelorette parites, anniversaries, and birthdays.

Order #4000

The Joy of Parenthood
by Jan Blaustone

This treasury of wise and warm advice is an inspiration to parents. H. Jackson Brown, Jr. calls the book "a touching tribute to the joy of being a parent." Filled with poignant photographs.

Order #3500

Familiarity Breeds Children
The Best Quotes about Parenthood
Selected by Bruce Lansky

This collection of the cleverest and most outrageous things ever said about raising children makes an appealing gift for parents new and old.

Order #4015

Order Form

Quantity	Title	Author	Order No.	Unit Cost (U.S. $)	Total
	Age Happens	Lansky, Bruce	4025	$7.00	
	Best Baby Shower Book	Cooke, Courtney	1239	$7.00	
	Best Bridal Shower Party Game Book	Cooke, Courtney	6060	$3.95	
	Best Couple's Shower Party Game Book	Cooke, Courtney	6061	$3.95	
	Best Party Book	Warner, Penny	6089	$8.00	
	Familiarity Breeds Children	Lansky, Bruce	4015	$7.00	
	For Better And For Worse	Lansky, Bruce	4000	$7.00	
	Grandma Knows Best	McBride, Mary	4009	$7.00	
	Joy of Friendship	Scotellaro, Robert	3506	$7.00	
	Joy of Grandparenting	Sherins/Holleman	3502	$7.00	
	Joy of Marriage	Dodds, Monica/Bill	3504	$7.00	
	Joy of Parenthood	Blaustone, Jan	3500	$7.00	
	Kids' Holiday Fun	Warner, Penny	6000	$12.00	
	Kids' Party Games and Activities	Warner, Penny	6095	$12.00	
	Lovesick	Lansky, Bruce	4045	$7.00	
	Very Best Baby Name Book	Lansky, Bruce	1030	$8.00	
				Subtotal	
			Shipping and Handling (see below)		
			MN residents add 6.5% sales tax		
				Total	

YES, please send me the books indicated above. Add $2.00 shipping and handling for the first book and 50¢ for each additional book. Add $2.50 to total for books shipped to Canada. Overseas postage will be billed. Allow up to four weeks for delivery. Send check or money order payable to Meadowbrook Press. No cash or COD's please. Prices subject to change without notice. **Quantity discounts available upon request.**

Send book(s) to:

Name _____ Phone _____

Address _____

City _____ State _____ Zip _____

Payment via:

❑ Check or money order payable to Meadowbrook Press. (No cash or COD's please.) Amount enclosed $_____

❑ Visa (for orders over $10.00 only)   ❑ MasterCard (for orders over $10.00 only)

Account # _____ Signature _____ Exp. Date _____

A **FREE** Meadowbrook Press catalog is available upon request.
You can also phone us for orders of $10.00 or more at 1-800-338-2232.

Mail to: Meadowbrook Press
5451 Smetana Drive, Minnetonka, MN 55343
Toll-Free 1-800-338-2232

Phone (612) 930-1100   Fax (612) 930-1940